D1191512

LET IT GO!

EMILY MORGAN

LET
IT
GO!

How to *(Finally)* Master Delegation
& Scale Freedom Across Your Organization

HOUNDSTOOTH
PRESS

LET IT GO!

How to (Finally) Master Delegation & Scale Freedom
Across Your Organization

ISBN   978-1-5445-3066-6 *Hardcover*
   978-1-5445-3065-9 *Paperback*
   978-1-5445-3067-3 *Ebook*

To the leader I supported early on, Joe Sun,
who first taught me about delegation
and letting go.

And to the leaders that followed,
who let me learn and then lead them on the
journey to delegation self-mastery.

And always, to my son Nathan,
who continues to remind me that none of
my work would exist without him.
And, he's right!

CONTENTS

INTRODUCTION 1

PART 1
MINDSET

CHAPTER 1
**STEP 1: KNOW YOUR
MOST IMPACTFUL CONTRIBUTION** 7

CHAPTER 2
STEP 2: REPROGRAM YOUR VALUE 21

CHAPTER 3
STEP 3: SHIFT YOUR MINDSET 33

PART 2
TECHNIQUE

CHAPTER 4
THE DISCIPLINE 47

CHAPTER 5
THE ART 81

CHAPTER 6
THE SCIENCE 101

PART 3
EXECUTION

CHAPTER 7
**RELIABLE AND REPEATABLE
DELEGATION** 117

CHAPTER 8
**THE TEN HABITS AND MINDSETS
OF ELEVATED LEADERS**. 141

CHAPTER 9
CASCADING A CULTURE OF DELEGATION 161

CONCLUSION 173

INTRODUCTION

This book is about learning how to finally let go of the work that holds you and your team back from making your collective most impactful contribution. I firmly believe that as leaders, we are each put into the world to make an impactful contribution that only we can make. In my work I have found that delegation is the tool you can use to create the space you need to live out this mission and foster a *culture of delegation™* that starts with you. What I mean by culture of delegation is the deep-seated value your organization places on the effective distribution of responsibilities and tasks to achieve your company's vision and goals.

My journey with delegation has evolved over time. I spent my early career working as an executive assistant, supporting others in various capacities and organizations where I was delegated to. Years later, when I started my delegation company, I was both the entrepreneur and the assistant. I was servicing clients, learning how to be an entrepreneur, building out my business, and learning how to delegate to others.

My view on delegation is a 360-degree deep dive. I've been both a career "delegator" and a career "delegatee." At the printing of this book, I will have spent fifteen years running a delegation company where we have helped hundreds of entrepreneurs save tens of thousands of hours by teaching them how to "let it go" and increase their freedom and impact to do incredible work in the world. The thoughts, concepts, and solutions shared in this book are a culmination of both my experience as an award-winning entrepreneur running a delegation company and my work supporting the nation's top entrepreneurs.

As leaders, our teams and stakeholders are counting on us to show up each day with the strength and clarity required to make our biggest and most impactful contribution. The only way we can do this is by continuing to elevate ourselves through awareness, and intentionally conserving our time, energy, and focus. I'm convinced that the single best way to do this is through a fanatical and consistent commitment to delegation.

Delegation is deep work. It's hard work, but delegation is the foundation for the growth that creates freedom for you and your company. Once you master it, you teach and empower your team to master it. Through this commitment of letting go, the entire organization shifts into a team of people doing meaningful work that they love. They are happier in their work and stay in their jobs longer, and your company can make a bigger impact than you ever dreamed possible doing it all on your own.

This is the vision of a delegation culture. It's a retention strategy, a salvation strategy, and an impact strategy that you can implement within your business today to produce results. All it takes is an open mind, an open heart, and a willingness to go deep and think differently about delegation and what we are ultimately here to contribute.

I've structured the book in three parts with three chapters in each part. In Part 1, we start with the essential three steps to reframe your mindset. In my experience helping hundreds of entrepreneurs to delegate over the years, these three steps are the missing link for being able to delegate well.

Once you've done the deep work in Part 1, you'll learn the techniques for how to delegate in Part 2. This is the tactical side of delegation, consisting of three important components: the art, science, and discipline of delegation. All three must work together seamlessly for you to be able to feel the impact that delegation can bring.

In Part 3, it all comes together in execution. When you are right with yourself, and have developed the mindset and technique to delegate well, you can then start to cascade a culture of delegation through your team.

To help you on your journey, all resources discussed in this book can be found at our website, letitgodelegationbook.com. ⓘ

This book isn't about what you've done wrong in the past, but how you can enjoy the freedom of delegating with the confidence to finally do it right. I get the frustration many business leaders feel, because I've been there and I understand the scar tissue you may have developed around delegation. It's time to put that all aside as I take your hand on this transformational journey to achieving effective, impactful delegation.

Mindset. Technique. Execution. This is your formula for success.

Are you ready? Let's do this.

PART 1

MINDSET

*"All great changes
are preceded by chaos."*

—DEEPAK CHOPRA

CHAPTER 1

STEP 1·
KNOW YOUR MOST
IMPACTFUL CONTRIBUTION

"I am mine, before I am ever anyone else's."

—Nayyirah Waheed

I firmly believe that each of us is here to make a special contribution that only we can make. When we know what our calling is, we find ourselves in the zone, overflowing with passion, excitement, and energy. In life and in work, your ability to identify, stay in touch with, and articulate your own most impactful contribution is the key to finding limitless freedom and to maximizing your purpose. It's what I call an "elevated" state of mind and time.

The world needs each of us to bring our talents, deepest passions, and boundless energy to accomplish the special things we are uniquely suited to do. Unfortunately, as we build our businesses, careers, and lives, all too many of us lose sight of our own special abilities, as well as the talents of others around us, and how to best apply them to meet our goals.

In my business career, I've found that strategic delegation of work is the primary tool to get you from where you and your organization are now to where you're meant to be. Delegation is vital because the world needs each of us to elevate our time and energies to innovate and accomplish our objectives.

As your business evolves, you may find yourself holding a death grip on work that others could handle as well as or even better than you. Yet somehow you just can't let go. In our work at Delegate Solutions, we fight this battle every day with the entrepreneurs we advise.

For example, take our client Henry. As he moved from a solopreneur to having a small team, he struggled with being able to let go of his day-to-day tasks. At times this came across as being hypercritical because he was micromanaging his team to excess, always wanting to oversee every little detail of his business. He wanted to review everything he had delegated with a fine-tooth comb, including social media posts, order forms, and email responses, simply because until that moment he'd been the only person who had ever handled those tasks. However, our team was able to slowly build trust over time through consistent execution and care to gently force him out of those habits and elevate himself as the *visionary* of his company.

There are many reasons why my team and I are determined to help business leaders let go of their death grip on work. We have seen that some leaders have become used to attributing their value and contribution to how busy they are, and they become more concerned with their output, rather than their impact. Entrepreneurs can become very comfortable in "busyness," so much so that they can potentially spend their entire careers attending to tasks because it becomes a safe, comfortable space and makes them feel useful.

As our teams grow and evolve, if we aren't careful, we can start to settle in and slowly assume the persona of being the "hero" of our companies. We find ourselves getting rushes of dopamine from being regarded as the one who swoops in to solve every single problem in our companies. We can get pleasure from the feeling of being needed all the time. We may subconsciously even start to feel so energized by being the hero, or bored by what we are doing each day, that we actually start creating the messes and fires in our business to keep the adrenaline flowing.

Perhaps you've met a woman like Sue. She's always running around like her hair is on fire. She's triple-booked every day, and makes promises she can't keep because she's too busy to execute on anything. Her team is endlessly turning over because they have to spend the majority of their time cleaning up her messes, and they are powerless to change it.

Like Sue, many of us are so overwhelmed with the busyness of our business that we've lost touch with *what* we really wanted to spend our time on. We've been distracted from what we originally felt called to do, and from the impact we wanted to make through work and in our personal lives. We find ourselves all too comfortable and busy doing work that sucks the life out of us, and we can find ourselves stuck here.

People follow their leaders to the extent that companies become so busy executing that no one is innovating. This is because the someone who should be innovating is *you*, but you're so busy saving the day, or ordering all of the office supplies, that you're missing opportunities to make a real impact. We *must* find ways to shift our own thinking to value the ideas we have over the tasks we do.

I've learned over the years that a company without a visionary creates a vacuum, and can die from lack of innovation. Your ability to connect with, value, and articulate your most impactful contribution creates a lens from which all delegation extends. It forces you to be clear on what you want to spend your time and energy on *before* you start to delegate. This lens helps you quickly and easily filter out activities that are out of alignment with your most important work and allows you to easily spot possible delegations more clearly than you could before.

When you focus on valuing and embracing your most impactful contribution—when you truly understand it and create boundaries to protect it—then you are finally ready to delegate. The clarity that comes with understanding what you want to spend your time on allows you to clearly spot all the things you are missing, and gives you a roadmap to freedom.

In the past, your delegations may have occurred haphazardly, impulsively, and without much thought. You may feel that delegation hasn't really moved the needle for you in relation to the time you were able to free up. That's likely because the delegation only created a vacuum of time for you, where the time saved through delegation just got refilled with more busy work.

Parkinson's Law applies here: "*Work expands to fill the time we allow to complete it.*" For delegation to work well and for you to finally let go, you *first* have to bring clarity to what you want to do with the time you free up, and then start to delegate from there.

A DELEGATION TALE

Meet Tom. We will follow his delegation journey as we work through this book. Tom decided on a whim after talking to a friend that he needed an assistant to help him clear his plate. He excitedly hired Anne very quickly without any real delegation plan. By the time Anne started, Tom's excitement had shifted to other new projects and priorities, and he spent only a few minutes with Anne in those first few days. Anne spent the majority of her first two weeks waiting to catch Tom after his meetings to ask him to give her things to do, as they never agreed to any sort of regular meeting cadence to check in.

Tom's first problem was that he had never really thought through how he wanted to spend the time he freed up by hiring Anne. He just knew he had to clear his plate, thought it would be cool to have an assistant, and excitedly made the hire. He was able to initially hand over a few tasks, but found himself getting endlessly frustrated that Anne kept coming to him with a bunch of questions. She was supposed to make his life easier, not harder, right? On top of that, he was growing frustrated that Anne didn't seem to have much to do, and she kept putting most of the things she completed back on his desk for him to review, which only added to his stress. So now, not only was Tom drowning in even more busy work, but the time he was able to free up by hiring Anne was spent in frustration and distraction.

In contrast, Tom could have hired an assistant only after an exhaustive search. Before the assistant started, he could have made a list of all the work he was doing, and gotten clear on what he really wanted to do instead. He would have then devoted an hour-long meeting each day with his assistant Anne to systematically delegate work and clear his plate. They would have added time blocks to Tom's calendar and set up an ongoing time to meet at the end of each day to assess what was accomplished or required Tom's feedback.

This deliberate and focused approach to delegation would have made all the difference for Tom. To delegate well, he needed to be clear on what he wanted to hand off, and make time each day to connect with his assistant. He also would have had a plan for how he wanted to use the time he freed up.

In the coming chapters we'll follow Tom on his delegation journey and see how he makes out.

YOUR TURN

Before you start to think about what and how to delegate, let's start with *why*. In the following exercise, you will work to uncover *your* own most impactful contribution, which must be the foundation of your delegation strategy. The goal here is to get back in touch with your why and understand what you really want to contribute.

In the exercise, I'll ask you to attach "feeling" adjectives that align with each question or statement. When we put words to emotions, we create an emotional attachment to our thoughts. The more we can see and feel our vision, the easier it will be to execute.

It's important to note that others see things in us that we don't see in ourselves. Because thoughts and feelings come naturally to us, we view them as normal and not unique, but they are really exceptional parts of us. As you go through this process, think back on any positive feedback others may have shared with you that could be possible themes about why you're here and what makes you unique. Here we go.

1. What are some of your favorite things to do, personally or professionally, that bring you a lot of energy? These are things you could spend all day doing.

   a. _____

   b. _____

   c. _____

2. How does it make you feel when you do these things?

   a. _____

   b. _____

   c. _____

What follows is a "feeling wheel" to help you select adjectives that feel right to you as you work through each item.

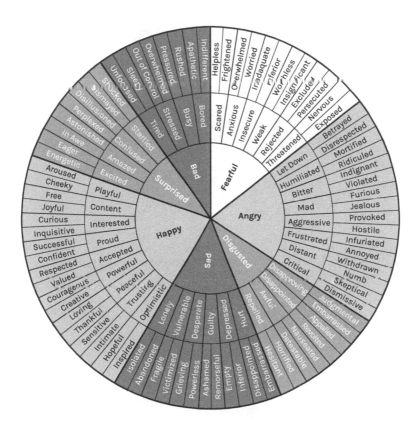

Feeling Wheel of adjectives.

3. I've heard people tell me over the years that I'm really great at:

   a. _____

b. _____

c. _____

4. When people tell me what I'm great at, I feel
   (*insert adjectives*):

   a. _____

   b. _____

   c. _____

Let's get deeper into work:

1. When it comes to my work, my ideal day would be spent
   doing:

   a. _____

   b. _____

   c. _____

2. When I'm spending time doing these things, I feel
   (*insert adjectives*):

   a. _____

   b. _____

   c. _____

3. I feel like I can make the biggest impact in my work each day by doing:

   a. _____

   b. _____

   c. _____

4. When I think about being able to spend my time doing these impactful things, I feel *(insert adjectives)*:

   a. _____

   b. _____

   c. _____

5. Why do I want to do these things?

   a. _____

   b. _____

   c. _____

6. Why are they so important to me?

   a. _____

   b. _____

   c. _____

7. What impact will I make by doing them?

a. _____

b. _____

c. _____

You should see a lot of positive emotions reflected in this exercise. We always want to start with the positive and find ways to expand on it. This helps create a clear headspace for us to begin to connect the emotion to the associated activities.

Based on your answers above:

1. What trends do you see in how you want to spend your time each day?

2. What do you think you are called to do with your life?

3. What impact do you want to make?

4. What do you see as your most impactful contribution?

As I learn to delegate more to elevate myself out of the day to day, I will spend my newfound time on:

1. _____

2. _____

3. _____

What impact will you be able to make with this new focus?

_____

_____

_____

_____

Congratulations, you are now cleared for delegation takeoff! You may proceed through the rest of the book.

CHAPTER 2

STEP 2:
REPROGRAM YOUR VALUE

"Try not to become a man of success.
Rather become a man of value."

—ALBERT EINSTEIN

On his delegation journey, Tom spent much of his first few weeks fumbling through delegating work to his new assistant Anne. He would find a task that he thought was boring and lob it over to her without much thought or consideration for her need for details. He was still busy running around putting out fires, and wasn't invested in spending any time with her to explain things, or answering questions that she had regarding the work she was asked to do. He saw the tasks as low-value activities, and eventually parts of them wound up back on his plate for him to handle anyway, which only added to his frustration.

The truth is, there were many reasons that Tom was holding back, which have nothing to do with delegation, as we'll see in later chapters. Some reasons are cultural, relational, economic, emotional, and psychological, and they can stop us in our tracks from taking any steps forward into more freedom. Like Tom, many of us have never really thought about what our time is worth, or gone very deep into what we want to spend our time on, or created measurements to evaluate how we should spend it.

Some of us were brought up in an ingrained culture where working ourselves to the bone is the standard. A culture where burning the midnight oil, doing everyone else's job, and solving every single problem is a badge of honor and measure of success. We may have been taught that we must always be the first to arrive and last to leave, or we aren't contributing. Others may be so intimidated by the responsibility of how to actually achieve their big vision that they passively stay stuck in the comfort zone of busy work.

The weight of this has impacted our physical and mental health. Our relationships with our kids, friends, and families are suffering because our leading role as the "hardest worker" has made all other roles secondary. We've given up hobbies, birthdays, anniversaries, and workouts because there's always so much to do.

Therefore, the next step in delegation is about getting back in touch with your own value. If you can learn to spot, understand, and reprogram harmful thoughts, feelings, and behaviors, and work to unpack them, you can truly live the life you originally envisioned for yourself when you became a freedom-seeking entrepreneur.

It can be very easy to fall back on stories you've always told yourself about why you can't let go. In my work, I've heard all the excuses. Here are just a few:

- *"It's easier for me to do it myself than to explain it."*

- *"My work is too complicated to hand off."*

- *"I tried letting go before and it got screwed up and cost me more time to fix it."*

- And, my favorite, *"I know I need help, but I don't even think I'm in a place where I can bring someone in yet."*

Do some of these resonate with you? The fact is, while these emotions are real, deep, and raw, all of the statements above are simply self sabotaging thoughts that keep us stuck. Recognizing your patterns and what lies behind them is the first step toward changing your heart, mind, and behaviors to move forward.

FIVE REASONS
WE SELF-SABOTAGE

According to leading researchers in the space of mental health, there are five key reasons we self-sabotage:

1. Fear

You may have a fear of failing or even a fear of being successful, which may seem unusual but happens when the path to success is stressful. It's not uncommon for people to fear what will happen when they finally achieve a goal, so they will engage in behaviors that make the achievement more difficult or unlikely.

2. Insecurities

Self-sabotaging may occur when a person doesn't feel confident or worthy enough to find happiness or achieve a goal. Insecurities keep people from pushing forward and reduce motivation.

3. Need for Control

The uncertainty of new outcomes can make people uncomfortable, leading to self-sabotaging behaviors that bring them back to more "comfortable" situations [in which they feel more in control]. In this case, comfort is simply a place or emotion they've experienced before, even if it's negative.

4. Placing Blame

If you are quick to point fingers every time something goes wrong, then you may be self-sabotaging by placing blame instead of taking responsibility or realizing that sometimes things just don't go as planned. Plus, placing blame on others doesn't allow you to learn and grow from challenging situations.

5. Procrastination

It's not uncommon to stall or hesitate before beginning an important task. This can be a reaction to fear or lack of motivation, but procrastinating is a type of self-sabotage.[1]

Research also shows that self-sabotage typically happens when we are looking for a way out.[2] These behaviors suggest that something about our situation isn't working. Typically, when we are trying to delegate, we are at our max and looking to get away from work that is slowing us down. This dynamic makes us prone to self-sabotaging delegation behavior, simply because we are at a place where we are trying to break through.

Entrepreneurs in particular can suffer from an additional layer of emotional complexity that I refer to as "founders' syndrome." In my

---

[1] Christine Ruggeri, "What Causes Self-Sabotaging Behaviors? (And How Do You Stop?)," Dr. Axe, July 3, 2021, https://draxe.com/health/self-sabotaging/.

[2] Crystal Raypole, "How Self-Sabotage Holds You Back," Healthline, October 22, 2021, https://www.healthline.com/health/self-sabotage.

extensive work trying to help clients delegate to elevate their time and finally let go, they've shared thoughts such as:

- "*I feel guilty or weak asking others to do things to help me.*"

In cases like this, a leader may have had to prove themselves to a family member or old boss by being the first to arrive and last to leave to show their commitment. They were never able to ask for any help and were never offered any. There's a deep sense of pride that comes from "doing it all myself" and finding success in that, but we can become stuck in a negative thought pattern in which asking for help is viewed as a weakness. Not viewing our time as valuable or ourselves as worthy of help can have roots in family and culture.

- "*I hate and naturally resist systems, discipline, and structure.*"

Free-spirited entrepreneurs love making this statement. It's almost become a badge of honor in the entrepreneurial community to make this claim, as if we are some sort of vigilante "barn burners" because we naturally resist structure. The assumption is that by subscribing to any level of systematization, we are conforming to societal norms, which are not allowing us to be special or unique. However, the greatest entrepreneurs of our time built their empires by being hyperdisciplined instead.

- *"I secretly like the rush and energy I create when I start or put out fires."*

This is likely one that is not said out loud, nor is there typically any initial awareness of this dynamic, which requires significant self-reflection. When we dig deep within ourselves and our behaviors, however, it's easy to spot the trends. A lot of the time, this pattern occurs because the leader has lost touch with their vision and is trying to get reenergized in other ways that happen to be destructive.

- *"I'm scared that I will be seen as a fraud if someone is doing things as well or better than me."*

Leaders who make this type of statement have a fear of letting go. They are afraid that if they let go of tasks and projects and start to delegate, others will say, "That's really easy, that's not special." So, they choose to instead hold tight and hoard tasks to maintain their sense of contribution.

- *"I haven't earned this freedom yet."*

All the rugged individualists out there are groaning over this one. (I can literally hear you!) We believe we got to where we are because of all the hard work we put in, all the sleepless nights, "attaboys," and last-minute miracles we pulled off, and we are proud to say that we did it all on our own. We haven't yet earned the right to have free time to ideate, relax, or delegate. We just aren't "there" yet.

Reading the statements above may feel as though you are looking in a mirror. And whether the thoughts are based in reality or fear, they are the real words of entrepreneurs I've worked with over the years who found themselves stuck and unable to delegate. The key is to spot and unpack the self-sabotaging thoughts so that you can move past them.

UNPACKING EXERCISE

Here's an exercise to help you begin to unpack.

What are some self-sabotaging thoughts you may have said to yourself when it comes to being able to let go?

_____

_____

_____

Why do you think you might have been stuck in these patterns or thoughts? Think about any cultural, economic, emotional, relational, or psychological reasons that might be influencing you.

_____

_____

_____

UNDERSTANDING YOUR WORTH

The last piece to reprogramming your value is to really put a dollar amount to your time so that you can make better, more educated, and intentional decisions about how you use it. In my work, I've found that our ability to truly let go has a direct correlation to how we value our time. Let's do some quick math on what your time is currently worth that you can use as a baseline to start from.

Using the following formula, find your hourly rate. You can base this on your current salary or your future ideal salary. For example: if your annual salary is $250k and you are ideally working an average of forty hours a week, that equates to $120/hour.

You can do your own math here:

- Annual salary: $_____

- Divide by 2,080 hours (forty hours/week)

- Your hourly rate is: $_____

Save this number, we will reference it in a later chapter!

This number should be an eye-opener to you as a real data point for the types of things you're spending your time on. Are they $120/hour tasks? Likely not. If we insist on being the wearer of all the hats, we will continue to load our plates with work that others can do, perhaps better than we can, and we'll spend a fortune paying ourselves to do it.

This chronic behavior of overcommitment and not letting go is costing us time, money, and energy. According to the *Harvard Business Review*,[3] which surveyed more than 400 executives, business owners, and entrepreneurs, the average business leader was working a seventy-two-hour week. A Gallup and Wells Fargo poll found that 57 percent of small business owners work six days a week. And over 20 percent of them work seven days a week.

A similar study looked at the work habits of business owners and their key executives and found that they spent more than 30 percent (one-third!) of their workweeks on time-wasting, low-value, and no-value activities that added little to no value to their companies.[4]

A third of our time is wasted! What could you do with an extra 30 percent more time in your week?

Remember, creep is real. Once you have an awareness of what you want to spend your time on, and use delegation to strategically clear

---

[3] Jennifer J. Deal, "Welcome to the 72-Hour Work Week," Harvard Business Review, September 12, 2013, https://hbr.org/2013/09/welcome-to-the-72-hour-work-we.

[4] David Finkel, "New Study Shows You're Wasting 21.8 hours a Week," Inc., March 1, 2018, https://www.inc.com/david-finkel/new-study-shows-youre-wasting-218-hours-a-week.html.

everything else from your plate, you create space and breathing room in your life. Parkinson's Law rules here. "Work expands to fill the time we assign it." If you aren't careful and intentional, you can quickly create a vacuum of time that gets refilled with more easy, but low-value, activities. If your schedule is not vigorously protected, time vampires can slowly start to creep back in and steal back precious moments of your newfound time.

RECAP

Let's take a moment to recap and build on what we've covered so far.

1. Step 1 (from Chapter 1)

   a. My most impactful contribution is: _____

   _____

   b. When I free up my time, I want to spend it on:

      i. _____

      ii. _____

      iii. _____

   c. The impact I will make by doing these things (my why) is:

   _____

2. Step 2 (from Chapter 2)

    a. Look back at the Worth Formula we calculated above
       and place that number below:

        i. My hourly rate is: $_____.

        ii. I will reference this data point as I make decisions
            around what is coming off my plate and ask myself
            if the tasks that I am doing are that dollar value.

Now that you've explored your most impactful contribution and
your value, it's time to move on to shifting your mindset.

CHAPTER 3

STEP 3:
SHIFT YOUR MINDSET

"What you think, you become."

—The Buddha

Many years ago, when I was going through a really challenging time in my personal life, I discovered meditation. I had hit a roadblock that I couldn't see how to get through mentally and emotionally. I was stuck in some self-sabotaging behavior that required me to find a fresh mindset and perspective. Meditation and affirmations helped me create space in my mind and change my thinking about how to move forward.

In my meditation practice, I learned the concept that what we focus on expands, and the stories we tell ourselves are the stories we believe, even if they are false narratives. I have seen this play out in so many ways for myself and so many others time and again.

All the work that you've done in the previous two chapters has set the stage for developing a mindset that's healthy and ready for delegation. In this chapter, we'll delve into the process of shifting your mindset for transformational change through delegation.

As Carol Dweck says in *Mindset: The New Psychology of Success*, "Becoming is better than being." We are each on a journey of self-enlightenment to becoming better delegators. However, I've found in my work that in most delegation conversations, people are talking about the wrong things. Delegation is actually very deep work that unfortunately gets glossed over in the typical business environment.

Most of us are constantly told that we "should" delegate, and we are taught techniques for "how" to delegate, but the fundamental issues of why we struggle with delegation are never acknowledged, addressed, or worked through. So, we start to view delegation as a chore, rather than a choice. And our failed attempts at delegation begin to compound, cloud, and complicate our own thinking about delegation. In the end, we simply stop trying.

Think back to Tom and his failed attempt at delegation. Let's look deeper into his personal backstory. Tom hired Anne quickly and on a whim. His friend had recently hired an assistant and was bragging about how great it was. Tom is someone who prides himself on making decisions quickly and getting things moving, so he made the jump to hire his assistant Anne without much thought. He soon felt himself hanging on to work rather than delegating, because he was stuck in old patterns of needing to feel busy all of the time. He was concerned that, if he started handing all of his work to Anne, he wouldn't have anything to do. What would be his value to the company? That fear stopped him because he had never let himself think about alternatives, so he held on to the work to remain "busy." It was his go-to narrative, the story of his life.

Tom's father was a first-generation immigrant who had started his company from nothing thirty years earlier. The company had experienced tremendous success and the founder's dream was always to retire and pass the business to his son. Tom wanted to please his father so he jumped in to help run the company when he was just twenty-five. He did whatever his father asked of him and prided himself on being the first person everyone called to solve a problem. Toilet clogged? Call Tom. Shipments delayed? Call Tom. Angry customer? Call Tom. He enjoyed feeling useful by doing whatever was needed.

Tom hadn't spent a lot of time with his father when growing up, because his dad was always working. So he thought that by joining the business he could spend more quality time with his father and make him proud. The firefighting came naturally to Tom, so he proudly dove in, even if it wasn't fulfilling work. After every problem was solved, and every fire put out, Tom's dad would give him an "attaboy," which validated Tom's contribution as the wearer of many important hats. With his dad at the helm, however, Tom was never asked to work on the big vision for the company. His value, as determined by his father, was cleaning up messes and putting out fires, and Tom was comfortable there.

The problem was that Tom wasn't feeling personally satisfied or purposeful in his work. One of the reasons he hired Anne was to help alleviate some of the tasks that made him feel bored.

When Tom stepped in to join the company, he was under tremendous pressure from his dad to put in the same long hours and prove that he was ready to take the wheel. If Tom didn't appear busy all of the time, his dad would tease him and call him a slacker. This deep-seated need to please his dad and live out his father's legacy kept him from ever really thinking about what he wanted his own legacy to be. So, he stayed busy doing all the things that were asked of him.

Tom was initially very excited to have an assistant, until his father joked that Tom didn't need any help, he just needed to work as hard as his dad had worked to build the company from scratch. But soon after Tom hired Anne, his dad became sick and died shortly thereafter. Tom was on his own, and he began to feel tremendous guilt and shame about hiring an assistant. He was deeply conflicted about letting down his father's memory by not working hard enough. This continued to impact his ability to give any substantial work to Anne.

His situation was compounded by the fact that he lacked vision for what he actually wanted to spend his time on. He'd always gotten by doing the busy work of putting out fires, but with his father gone everything—including the vision for the company—now fell to him. He felt ill-prepared and was consumed with self-doubt. Tom's situation and emotions had him stuck, and without consistent delegation from Tom, Anne was left feeling helpless, frustrated, and confused.

These kinds of situations are playing out in companies around the country every single day. Each storyline is different but the themes are the same. As we saw in Chapter 2, there are so many reasons we struggle with delegation, including emotional, relational, and psychological factors. That's why in this book, we are starting with the deep work to clear the way for effective delegation.

Most speakers on this topic will teach you best practices for delegation, but my guess is that it hasn't moved the needle for you so far. That's because we need to solve the root issues within ourselves first to free ourselves to delegate effectively. In truth, our struggle with delegation is not actually a business issue, it's a human behavioral issue. We are stuck because we are telling ourselves the wrong stories.

Entrepreneurs are energized and motivated by freedom, so it's simply not sustainable to leave our challenges with delegation unsolved. They are holding us back, slowing us down, and keeping us from making the impact we are here to bring to the world. And they are impacting those around us who simply want to contribute, do a good job, and help us succeed.

REFRAME
YOUR THINKING

To shift our mindsets for delegation, we need to reframe our thinking. It starts with reframing the negative beliefs and stories we tell ourselves with a narrative that's more positive and self-fulfilling.

In the example of Tom, instead of telling himself that delegating is a sign of weakness, he might say something like, "Delegation helps me free up my time and energy to do my most impactful work." Of course, Tom still has personal work to do to figure out what his most impactful contribution is, but he can start by recognizing thoughts that don't serve him, and reframing those negative beliefs with positive statements to begin shifting his mindset.

We'll leave Tom for now as we go deeper into mindset and the technique of delegation in Part 2. Then, in Chapter 8, we'll come back to Tom's delegation journey when we explore The Ten Habits and Mindsets of Elevated Leaders.

As you move through this book, you are building your clarity and positive thoughts into your own cohesive and powerful story that will change your heart and mind. Our brains are able to modify thoughts and our ability to grow and learn by harnessing the power of "neuroplasticity." We can train our brains to acquire new habits around any changes we desire through a series of attention, reward, and reinforcement behaviors, such as focusing on the positive through reflection and affirmation.

Through the thoughtful use of small, consistent behavioral changes, we can create big transformations. These are the principles we will apply in our approach to changing your heart and mind around delegation, which will allow you to reclaim your energy and passion for what you do.

> When asked what the biggest mistake is that people make in life, the Buddha replied, "The biggest mistake is you think you have time. Time is free but it's priceless. You can't own it but you can use it. You can't keep it but you can spend it. And once it's lost you can never get it back."

Ultimately, your time and energy as a leader are all you've got to work with. Your team and the world in general are relying on you to maintain and protect your energy so that you can keep creating and innovating. In fact, once you have mastered delegation you can multiply your impact tenfold if you can get your team leveraged and encourage them to delegate and elevate themselves alongside you. Imagine the impact of a culture where an entire organization is delegating, elevating, innovating, and executing, free to explore and create because they have the energy available to do so. As a result, you can create jobs and solutions to impact some of the world's most complicated problems.

DELEGATION IS AN
ENERGY MANAGEMENT SYSTEM™

When you shift out of the default headspace of "I'm not a good delegator," and replace those negative thoughts with positive affirming ones, you create space for a positive mindset to move forward. You can then view delegation simply as a way to manage your energy. It's a way to shift from the tasks that drain you or don't serve your vision, and replace that time with higher-value activities.

Before starting this next exercise, look back at the last section of Chapter 2. Reconnect yourself with your most impactful contribution and your value, then start the exercise.

REFLECT: START WITH THE WINS

START WITH THE WINS

1. Write down an example of a delegation that went really well for you.

<table>
<tr>
<td></td>
<td>Example:

Our product launch kickoff party.</td>
</tr>
</table>

2. Why do you think it worked so well?

<table>
<tr>
<td></td>
<td>Example:

I just riffed on what I wanted it to be and someone else handled the details to get it done.</td>
</tr>
</table>

3. What were the key positive takeaways of that experience?

_____

_____

_____

AFFIRM:
REPEAT THE GOOD STUFF

Now, create an affirmation that you can repeat to yourself as you focus more on elevating yourself through delegation.

A few affirmation options follow, but feel free to create your own:

1. "Delegation comes easily and naturally to me and makes me feel _____." (Insert one of your positive adjectives from Chapter 1.)

2. "I am a _____ delegator!" (Insert one of your positive adjectives from Chapter 1.)

3. "My delegation efforts are being supported by the universe; my ideal day manifests into reality before my eyes." (Or, create your own affirmative statement.)

RECAP

Before moving on to Part 2 of the book, let's recap and build on what we've covered in Part 1.

1. Step 1 (from Chapter 1)

   a. My most impactful contribution is: _____

   _____

b. When I free up my time, I want to spend it on:

i. _____

ii. _____

iii. _____

c. The impact I will make by doing these things (my why) is:

_____

2. Step 2 (from Chapter 2)

a. My hourly rate is: $_____ and I will reference this data point as I decide what is coming off my plate.

b. I will reference this data point as I make decisions around what is coming off my plate and ask myself if the tasks that I am doing are that dollar value.

3. Step 3 (from Chapter 3)

My affirmation that I will repeat to myself when I start to feel negatively about letting go is: _____

_____

Now that you are clarifying your most impactful contribution, reprogramming your value, and shifting your mindset, you're ready for the tactical side of delegation: technique. Amazing work so far, you're on your way to becoming an incredible delegator!

PART 2

TECHNIQUE

"The most perfect technique is that which is not noticed at all."

—PABLO CASALS

CHAPTER 4

THE DISCIPLINE

"Whoever heeds discipline
shows the way to life."

—Proverbs 10:17

I n my work helping others master delegation, I've found that there are three components to the technique of delegating well: discipline, art, and science. When these three pieces work together in harmony, delegation abounds in a healthy, impactful way. In the following chapters, we'll work on the tactical side of delegation and learn techniques that we can apply to each of these three components. In this chapter, we start with discipline.

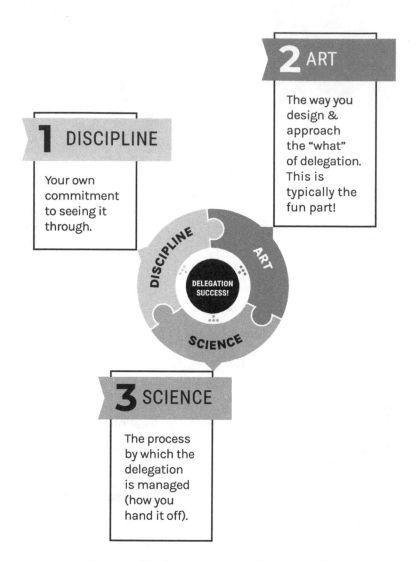

1 DISCIPLINE

Your own commitment to seeing it through.

2 ART

The way you design & approach the "what" of delegation. This is typically the fun part!

3 SCIENCE

The process by which the delegation is managed (how you hand it off).

DISCIPLINE

ART

SCIENCE

DELEGATION SUCCESS!

Technique: The three components of delegating well.

DISCIPLINE BEGINS WITH COMMITMENT

This is a *no judgment* chapter. With all the work you've completed in the earlier chapters, it's important to maintain a fresh, positive mindset as you work to become a better delegator. In this chapter, we will explore some of the behavioral aspects of delegation discipline that impact your ability to let go, and how to spot and address them.

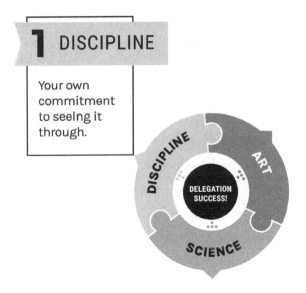

Discipline is your commitment to seeing delegation through.

The word "discipline" naturally brings about a negative emotion for many free-spirited leaders. But the ability to temper and leverage ourselves to achieve real, lasting progress is the mark of a game-changing entrepreneur. While this may be the hardest part of delegating well for many, it's the most important—especially if you have a vision for a culture of delegation that expands beyond you.

Discipline, in this context, is about our own focus and commitment to see things through. We need to understand that progress is more important than perfection. By making the commitment to finish what we started, even when we might lose interest at the end, we can finally make true progress.

You no doubt know a leader who relies on his luck and charisma to build his business. He puts on quite a show with big ideas, promises, and charm. What you don't likely see is the chaos that's being created backstage for his team in his wake. He may come across as a big idea guy, but leaves a trail of broken promises after each interaction. His team is confused, frustrated, and not aligned. His peers love his energy and big ideas, but they also know that they can't rely on him to see *anything* through that he commits to.

Delegation can help us deliver on promises if we are disciplined. If you want to be more than a glitzy show of one, it's important to bring both an understanding and awareness to your own behavioral tendencies. Remember, the world *needs* you and your big ideas.

Delegation is your path to help you and your team make those ideas a reality in a reliable and consistent way.

THREE BEHAVIORS OF A DISCIPLINED LEADER

In my work with entrepreneurs, I've found that there are three distinct behaviors present in a disciplined leader:

1. They respect systems and assigned seats.

In a growing company, confusion equals chaos. Disciplined leaders know that business scalability is based on strong systematization with a team executing consistently. They recognize that while they may have filled a particular seat in the past, they no longer sit there, and need to allow their assigned team to problem-solve accordingly in their seats. This commitment to the process and staying out of other people's way allows them to increase their leverage and impact, especially during periods of fast growth.

2. They are willing to be held accountable.

Disciplined leaders know that accountability starts at the top. Their commitment to lead by example is evident in their own ability to stay in their lane and respect the established plan of priorities. They appreciate having a team that holds them accountable to the stated vision and does not allow them to get distracted, even when they start to lose interest with the task at hand.

3. They temper themselves (and their new ideas!) for the greater good of their vision.

Disciplined leaders understand that growth, while exciting and validating, can easily disrupt their ability to focus on their single most valuable contribution: their vision. A company with endlessly preoccupied leadership cannot contribute in meaningful ways or sustain growth over time. This intentional commitment to not chase shiny objects once the plan is set creates a culture of focus and discipline.

* When you reflect on these three behaviors, how do you feel?

   _____

* Do you align or agree with them?

   _____

* Which one(s) do you struggle with the most?

   _____

- Is there one you do really well with, that you'd like to do even more with?

Remember, we are going for self-awareness, not judgment with this work.

FIVE BOTTLENECK
BEHAVIOR TYPES

With the ideal disciplined behaviors top of mind, let's explore the behaviors that can hinder a leader's ability to let go, and identify ways to overcome them. Keep in mind, we all exhibit one, some, or all of these behavior types at various times as leaders, and they are both psychological and emotional. Some are habits developed over time and some are hard-wired into us.

After more than fifteen years of helping others get better with delegation, I've identified the top five bottleneck behavior types that leaders exhibit. They are hero, interventionist, isolationist, time optimist, and dreamer.

The 5 Bottleneck Behaviors of Leaders

HERO

INTERVENTIONIST

ISOLATIONIST

TIME OPTIMIST

DREAMER

LET IT GO!

Putting a name to a type of behavior is powerful because it becomes so easy to spot and diagnose the behaviors objectively. For example, take Sam. Sam has an amazing, inspired personality and is always filled with new ideas. He loves to ideate and float in space with his ideas and needs to be pulled back down to earth most days. You can probably guess his type from the list above.

Sam is inspirational to be around, but can be frustrating to work with. His bottleneck tendency is to constantly share his ideas but never fully commit to one long enough to take it to the next level, or clearly define what success looks like to his team. Sam enjoys the energy of bouncing around starting fires, but they all inevitably burn out because he never gives sustained oxygen to any one idea. His tendency to frequently change his mind creates competing priorities for his team. They feel like they are always following him around while he chases the next shiny thing, which just leaves everyone feeling deflated because nothing is ever actually getting accomplished. We'll learn more about which behavior type Sam is exhibiting in the upcoming section.

Our ability to spot and name these kinds of behaviors, and put up some guardrails and awareness around them, allowed us to find a new level of freedom. To solve this, Sam's team learned to align with Sam around three specific priorities each week in their staff meeting. With this new focus, all of Sam's other ideas go onto a "parking lot" list of future ideas. When one of the projects gets completed, Sam selects the next priority from the parking lot and the team focuses on it with him. This simple shift in spotting and then working with Sam in a productive way based on his natural behavior style was highly effective, rather than always trying to keep up with a bunch of competing projects that never got finished.

What follows is an overview of each type (including Sam's!), how it happens, and how to resolve it.

Overview of Behavior Types

Type 1: The Hero—Always Wants to Save the Day

Summary

HERO

The Hero loves to save the day. If you're a Hero, your team has likely been conditioned to run everything through you for permission. Entrepreneurs are notorious for this type of behavior and as we discussed earlier, can sometimes attribute their own self-worth to this sense of feeling needed. They get energized by solving every issue within the business. A lot of the time, this behavior stems from a lack of process, accountability, and autonomy in your team. As I've let go of more and more myself, I've learned that sometimes this behavior stems from guilt around the transfer of work from my plate to someone else's.

How the Hero Affects the Team

Your team requires too much permission to execute and has to run too much through you. This stunts company growth. In some cases, the company is built starting from the ground up with the CEO being at the center of everything. Entrepreneurs are notorious for taking great pride in this position and begin to subconsciously thrive on the feelings of necessity and emergency that they receive from their team and their contribution to the business. Unfortunately, it's not a sustainable plan for growth and will never allow you to fully have a company that can run without your involvement if not addressed.

How It Happens

As the company grows, and processes are developed, steps are not taken to remove the CEO from the process. In many cases, your team has been conditioned to run everything through you. They require approval to take action, and need access and permission for information that only you know. It's also possible you haven't put the right resources in place (i.e., right people in the right seats) and there's a lack of clarity around roles and responsibilities because you haven't clearly mapped out processes with ownership. Because of the constant state of confusion, your team has become resistant to any new changes and may even begin "delegation blocking" just to remain relevant.

This behavior of delegation blocking can occur when your team hangs on to work to remain relevant. You may see it manifest itself as them interfering with something being handed off to someone else, or creating complexity around something being "too complicated" to delegate. Sometimes we exhibit this behavior ourselves for the same reasons. It can also be triggered by your own feelings of guilt as you step out of the really "hard" work. You may try to assuage your own guilt by "jumping in to help," which winds up stressing your team out even more.

Solutions for Heroes

1. Commit to extracting yourself. Take a hard look at parts of the business where you notice the team is still having to come to you. Try creating an inventory of your activities, especially looking at recurring processes to really identify what is still running through you that shouldn't be.

2. Grab some easy wins to build confidence for you and the team. Select a few small, easy processes that you notice

are a nuisance to you that are easy to capture and hand off. Write down the process as it is now and identify who is responsible for which step in the process. Wherever you see your name, replace it with another team member whenever possible.

3. Begin to verbally redirect your team to not include you in everything. They have been trained to come to you and they need to feel empowered and allowed to move things along without your constant involvement.

   Bonus! Having a designated gatekeeper for your time, who isn't you, helps this process. It's easier for someone who is not the CEO to tell them no. It may take a third party to break bad habits over time.

4. Start to delegate your thinking to your key team members. As you make decisions on things that they bring to you, explain *why* you approached it the way you did, and what thoughts influenced your decision. This allows them to attempt to make choices without you, or can at least minimize your overall involvement. Bonus points for starting every conversation with "What do you think we should do?" This allows both you and them to build confidence in *their* thinking.

Type 2: The Interventionist—Loves to Be in the Loop

Summary

INTERVENTIONIST

This type loves to always be looped in. It's my nice way of saying "micro-manager." Interventionists typically lack trust that anyone can do it as well as they can. Always feeling the need to intervene and constantly looking to tackle the full 80 percent instead of their 20 percent, they want to be in the loop at all times. Because of these high standards, they tend to "cocoon" to protect themselves from delegation errors of the past. Everything has been set up to require their participation to keep errors to a minimum. They are the de facto quality control officer.

How the Interventionist Affects the Team

You are continually involved in the 80 percent, rather than focusing on the 20 percent of most important work. You are not really committed to the delegation being successful because you haven't prepared the delegation properly, and do not trust the delegation process. This may stem from an "entrepreneurial hero" complex or just a general buildup of distrust in relying on other teammates.

Either way, a bad habit has developed of inserting yourself to remain in the loop at all times. Your constant need to control the outcomes frustrates your team and causes them to retreat from helping you, because they don't feel that their contribution matters.

How It Happens

We built this city! We built this city on you! Everything stems from you: your ideas, your plans, your vision, the sale, the execution. What you have built is largely reliant on your participation. You may have tried to find support in the past, and despite your best efforts, delegation failed. This has created a cocooning tendency around protecting yourself and your ideas from errors. You have not committed the time to make delegation successful or provided the clarity needed to execute to your standards. Because of this, you don't trust that anyone can do it as well as you can, and you insist on being part of everything going on in the business.

Solutions for Interventionists

1. Find the right support solution for yourself. Remember, if you don't have an assistant, you *are* the assistant! Struggles here could initially stem from an old staffing issue that broke down. If you didn't have the right resource in place in the past, you may have found yourself in a pattern of broken trust. It's also important to understand that strong administrative folks will always want to take action on

the next steps to your ideas. Be clear if you just want to bounce ideas and brainstorm with them rather than having them take action on something.

2. Once you have the right-fit support in place, take the time to delegate properly. Focus on sharing what success looks like for this project. Provide them with success criteria up front so that you create alignment. Share with them how this activity ties into the big picture and create accountability to put your mind at ease. Always establish who is doing what by when, and ensure that you set aside time to answer questions and for feedback.

3. Understand that, administratively, your work is not unique. A lot of the hesitation and frustration can stem from your own wrong assumptions that the delegation you are attempting is too complex and unique. A strong support partner will be able to separate the nuances from the core administrative process. I promise you, administratively speaking, the nuts and bolts of the work are always the same whether it's engineering, brain surgery, or running a marketing agency.

4. Restore your trust via an ongoing commitment to the process. Let a team member interview you to capture the process as you see it. Then let them help you tweak the process to make it run more smoothly. Respect that

not every person may tackle the steps in the same way and same order. You will need to let go and trust that your team will get to the final product in their own way. If it's a repeatable task or project, you will need to clearly define the project and explain if specific steps must happen in a specific order.

5. Start small to build trust. Try to create systems that include safety nets or ways for you to feel comfortable knowing that tasks are being handled properly. Know yourself. If you don't like to wait for updates or always assume the worst in situations, create working processes that help eliminate mental stress around delegating that will be a win-win as you start to let go sooner.

Type 3: The Isolationist—"I'll Just Do It Myself"

Summary

ISOLATIONIST

Isolationists love to say, "I'll just do it myself." It's become hard to delegate because you're doing everything yourself, and then you're not available to have key conversations with your team when you actually try to delegate something. It's impossible for your team to execute well because they don't have any opportunity to connect with you, which just spurs the cycle.

How the Isolationist Affects the Team

The established communication style across your team is holding you back and needs to be addressed. The team isn't clear on the process, or always requires additional details from you to complete projects. You aren't available to participate in the necessary conversations needed to see things through. You're too busy "doing" and are not being realistic about your time and involvement in the process, which is jamming up your team. You are not placing enough value on the time required to really delegate effectively. You will eventually find yourself quickly out of time, energy, and bandwidth.

How It Happens

Ah! You're completely overloaded and busting at the seams. You have complete awareness about how much help you need and have managed to find great help. There's just one problem: you have no time to spend with them to really make any traction. You're booked on back-to-back meetings all day, with no open windows to make time for the crucial conversations that are required to really move things forward on your behalf. Because you're so overwhelmed by your level of overcommitment, you provide minimal details to your team, have unrealistic expectations of turnaround time, and lack the time to close the loop on your portion of the delegations with your team.

Solutions for Isolationists

1. Prioritize and commit to a standing call or meeting each week or each day to be available to your team for questions. Set a clear agenda for what needs to get accomplished in these meetings so everyone knows in advance what information to prepare. Let your team be responsible for running those meetings and simply plan to show up and answer questions. Have your team repeat back to you what they heard and captured as priorities and align on next steps.

2. Establish a communication system that works for everyone on a consistent basis. Do you prefer to be asked questions as needed, or would you prefer them to lump together requests once per day? Commit to a certain level of responsiveness with your team.

3. Be sure you are creating a communication system that works for the reality of your day. It's fine to have goals and

hopes of evolving how you are managing this process. For now, just focus on finding a daily status update system that works to keep the delegation progressing with minimal commitment from you.

4. Be highly selective about your delegation. Focus on the most crucial things that need to move forward and commit to relaying details in an impactful way to your team. Take the small wins and build confidence and solid communication to help move things forward. Make the delegation as effective as possible by sharing your ideas for the success of the project with your team. This helps create alignment around expectations. You can even have your team interview you if you prefer to just verbally answer the questions, as opposed to having to write things out.

Type 4: The Time Optimist— Can Be Unrealistic About Time

I have to admit, if there's one behavior I struggle with, this is it! I am one of the most scheduled and structured leaders that I know, and I still have a tendency to be unrealistic with what can be done with the given time and resources.

Summary

TIME OPTIMIST

Time Optimists are overly optimistic by nature and can lack restraint when it comes to executing on only the best ideas. This behavior can create a lot of friction because your team is living in execution mode, and the competing messages from you confuse priorities in their already full days.

How the Time Optimist Affects the Team

You are overly optimistic about what can be accomplished with the staff and priorities you have. You have a lot of energy around your ideas, but sometimes lack restraint to only take action on your *best* ideas. Your team has become unfocused and confused because they are taking action on multiple things at once, and really aren't able to focus on the most crucial results of the day in an impactful way. This leads to burnout and frustration for everyone involved.

How It Happens

You are brilliant at developing new ideas and concepts, and your enthusiasm for accomplishment drives the energy of your team. Your team loves to help take action on ideas and bring them to life. The problem is that if everything is urgent, nothing gets done well because there's simply not enough time. This behavior of oversharing your ideas can also become toxic to your team, because they don't understand that sometimes you are just brainstorming and not even fully committed to the ideas you are sharing.

Solutions for Time Optimists

1. Create some awareness and boundaries for yourself. Understand that the people who support you, and hear your ideas and enthusiasm, believe it is their responsibility to help execute them. They too have limited time, and it can start to weigh on them if they can't keep up with your endless priorities. As you discuss delegations, have real conversations around how long it will take both you and the team to complete, and work together to prioritize the most impactful use of their time.

2. Establish priorities before you start to delegate. Understanding what the priorities are for the day, week, and month is always key for effectively supporting staff in handling those priorities. If they understand both your

objectives and priorities, they will accomplish the goals faster.

3. Align on who's doing what by when so that you are on the same page. Be clear on what the priority items are as well, so the team understands when it's okay to spend more time on one project or task versus another.

Type 5: The Dreamer—Loves to Ideate

Summary

DREAMER

Remember Sam from earlier in the chapter? This is his type. Dreamers love to ideate. Like the Time Optimist, this inclination to overload your team with your latest idea distracts and confuses them. Dreamers tend to not think through the execution or success criteria of their ideas in a way that allows them to be handed off well to their teams. Dreamers think everything past the new idea is boring and the ambiguity of any type of execution plan becomes a confidence killer for the team.

How the Dreamer Affects the Team

You haven't clearly defined what success in delegation looks like, which is making you unclear because you haven't thought about how to execute your ideas in much detail. This ambiguity is a recipe for disaster. You have a habit of changing your mind frequently as your ideas evolve. This will drive your team crazy, because they don't have what they need from you to properly take action on a project or idea. You are slowly chipping away at the impact, confidence, and productivity of your team to help you bring the ideas to life.

How It Happens

Your favorite place to hang out is in idea creation. No one does it better than you when it comes to having the courage to dream things up time after time. The challenge lies in the handoff of the information to the people who are there to help you bring it to life. What they need from you is clarity and commitment to see only your most important ideas through.

Solutions for Dreamers

1. Stop. Breathe. Reflect. Don't delegate unless you are clear that the work or project is important to you. Hold yourself to a requirement to always explain what success looks like, to test your idea, and to make sure you are clear on what

you want and what success looks like before you try to hand it off.

2. Restrain yourself from constant ideation to your team. Just understand that they live in execution as you are sharing your ideas.

3. Collaborate on what your vision entails and how you and your team can best bring it to fruition through trial and error. Have someone interview you to understand what success looks like and *why* it's important to you in the first place. This helps provide clarity for you and your support partners (team members to whom you delegate).

BOTTLENECK DIAGNOSTIC

This exercise is designed to help you understand which bottleneck behavior(s) you are exhibiting. Once you can diagnose, name, and spot the behavior type, you can create positive change for the behavior.

Please answer the following five questions to the best of your ability.

Type 1, Hero: which of the following statements best describes your current situation as it relates to your level of involvement in the day to day?

A. My team rarely involves me in the day-to-day ops. They have the autonomy, access, and knowledge to move things forward independently.

B. My team periodically must involve me in day-to-day ops. They understand roles and responsibilities and follow a process when it exists.

C. My team frequently involves me in day-to-day ops. They lack clarity on their roles, loosely follow a process, and always loop me in.

D. My team comes to me with questions every day. All communications and decisions run through me. We lack process and role responsibilities.

Type 2, Interventionist: which of the following statements best describes your current situation as it relates to your current delegation practice?

A. My team runs like a well-oiled machine. I delegate with ease and let them run with it. What comes back to me is at least at 80 percent complete.

B. I've had moderate success with delegating. I like to know what's going on, but don't need to be involved in every part of the process.

C. I want to manage and be involved in at least 75 percent of the decisions and projects. I have to stay on top of my team most of the time.

D. I always have to manage the details of what I hand off. I don't trust that it will be done to my standards. No one can do it as well as me.

Type 3, Isolationist: which of the following statements best describes your current situation as it relates to managing your priorities?

A. I meet with my team weekly to evaluate priorities and move forward with key projects. I make this crucial communication a priority.

B. My team has a general sense of priorities and we have a loose system in place to communicate each week. We have basic processes in place.

C. I can give my team minimal details, but can't find enough time to have crucial convos to actually move things forward without me.

D. I am completely overcommitted and don't have time to meet with my team on projects. My team is not clear on process or priorities.

Type 4, Time Optimist: which of the following statements best describes your current situation as it relates to your active projects?

    A. My team loves to help me bring my best ideas to life. We have a solid system to create alignment around expectations, so stuff gets done.

    B. I can typically relay my best ideas to my team in a way that they can take action and prioritize them. We could improve our project planning.

    C. My team feels unfocused around key priorities. We have not established a way to move things forward systematically.

    D. My team thinks all of my ideas and projects are urgent and can't prioritize them or help me understand realistic timelines to complete them.

Type 5, Dreamer: which of the following statements best describes your current situation as it relates to your ideas?

    A. I am disciplined to think through and commit to my best ideas. I'm thoughtful about how I hand them off to my team to take action.

    B. I'm pretty good about only sharing my best ideas with my team. I could do better with the level of detail I provide for them to take action.

C. I have a hard time keeping all of my ideas to myself. My team feels like they are running around, but we are not completing key projects.

D. Idea creation is what I do best. I tend to change my mind as my ideas evolve and it confuses my team because they don't know what to take action on.

How did you feel doing that exercise? Share three adjectives:

1. _____

2. _____

3. _____

Did any of those scenarios really strike a nerve for you? If so, which one and why?

_____

Now, let's analyze your results. If you selected C or D for any of the behavior types, you have tendencies toward that bottleneck type. Note those areas where you scored a C or a D by circling them.

- Type 1: Hero

- Type 2: Interventionist

- Type 3: Isolationist

- Type 4: Time Optimist

- Type 5: Dreamer

Not to worry if you scored Cs or Ds on all of them. We all vacillate through the different types at different times in our careers and even in our days! The goal here is to recognize our patterns, understand them, and then deploy solutions to modify behaviors to keep moving forward.

TIME TO REFLECT

Use the accompanying Time to Reflect "note chart" to sum up and reflect on the five behavioral types to deepen your understanding of how they may apply to you.

1. Which of the five behavioral types do you think you might be exhibiting most prominently and why?

<table>
<tr>
<td></td>
<td>Example:
100% Time Optimist!
I always think that I can get more done in a day than anyone else because I've had to rely on myself for so long. Now that I have a team, I forget that they are here to help me execute and have their own sets of skills to offer.</td>
</tr>
</table>

2. Is there a behavior type you struggled with in the past but have really mastered? How did you do that?

<table>
<tr>
<td></td>
<td>Example:
Interventionist.
As I've let go of more and more, I've built some trust. I also learned that sometimes you just need to get something "good enough" to keep things moving.</td>
</tr>
</table>

RECAP

Let's take a moment to recap and build on some of the essentials we've covered in the book so far:

1. Step 1 (from Chapter 1)

   My most impactful contribution is: _____
   _____

   a. When I free up my time, I want to spend it on:

      i. _____

      ii. _____

      iii. _____

   b. The impact I will make by doing these things (my why)
      is: _____

2. Step 2 (from Chapter 2)

   a. My hourly rate is: $_____ and I will reference
      this data point as I decide what is coming off
      my plate.

   b. I will reference this data point as I make decisions
      around what is coming off my plate and ask myself if
      the tasks that I am doing are that dollar value.

3. Step 3 (from Chapter 3)

   My affirmation that I will repeat to myself when I start to feel negatively about letting go is: _____

   _____

4. Step 4 (from Chapter 4)

   My most prominent bottleneck behavior type is: _____

   _____

   When I find myself exhibiting this behavior type, I will combat it by: _____.

With the discipline component of technique under our belts, we can move along to the next component: the art of technique.

CHAPTER 5

THE ART

> *"The creative process is one of*
> *surrender, not control."*
>
> —JULIA CAMERON

T he funny thing about delegation is that once you start doing it well, you just want to delegate more and more! It's liberating and exciting all at the same time. One of our clients, Mordecai, once described this feeling as being "a kid in the candy store."

The art of delegation is your opportunity to think creatively. Delegation can get overwhelming as you begin to realize just how much delegating you can do. It's important that we don't get stuck in the candy store trying to pick the perfect treat, because the art of delegation is where the magic happens.

The positive energy we create in delegating well is what will power us through all the delegation hurdles. Your path to freedom is now directly in front of you and you are chasing down that horizon, letting go of one task at a time.

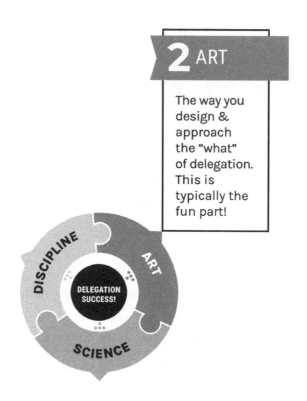

The art of delegation is the fun part.

And remember, as we discussed in earlier chapters, as you increase your level of delegation, it is really important to ensure that the space you are creating doesn't get refilled with more low-impact tasks. It's also important to ensure that what gets handed off actually moves the needle for you. In some cases, work we are currently doing shouldn't be on our plate or anyone else's plate because it can be automated or removed altogether.

BEST PRACTICES FOR THE ART

1. Always start with your goals: list them out, then work backward and ask yourself, *"What needs to happen for me to accomplish this goal? What do I specifically need to do to make this happen?"* Whatever is left, hand off.

   Tip! Use a support partner to add time blocks to your calendar to work on these activities. Or have them proactively prompt you for possible prep work to tee up your specific contribution to that goal.

2. Look for repeatables: this is always the easiest place to start with delegation. If it repeats and you're doing it, it needs to go. Have someone interview you on the process, capture it, and hand it off or automate it.

3. Find the low-hanging fruit: think about the things you do that are time wasters and things that need to get done but bring you no joy. Simple stuff like calling vendors, researching a gift, or finding a rental car. Use these to build your own confidence around delegation.

4. Compartmentalize: this one is key. I've seen many leaders get stuck here because they get overwhelmed when they try to think about handing off some big project or activity. Work with your support partner to help you break that big thing down into smaller chunks, and delegation will abound.

5. Use exercises: if you get stuck trying to figure out what to delegate, run some exercises that capture how you're spending your time. Next, I'll walk you through my favorite exercise.

Tip! For additional inspiration, check out our list of Sample Tasks to Delegate by category on our website at letitgodelegationbook.com. These are real tasks that we've done for clients and it's great for brainstorming when you get stuck.

FREEDOM ANALYSIS™ EXERCISE

With best practices in mind, let's explore what can come off your plate. This exercise is designed to help you objectively compartmentalize into buckets how your time is spent, so that you can take action quickly.

DELEGATION IS THE FOUNDATION FOR GROWTH.

In the exercise below, reflect on how you currently spend your time. Look back over the last few weeks and begin to list each activity in the appropriate section below.

Getting really clear on the most impactful use of your time is the key to creating a successful delegation strategy that actually brings you ROI, so start with #1 below.

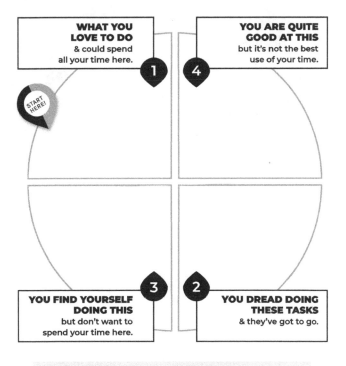

WHAT YOU LOVE TO DO
& could spend all your time here.

YOU ARE QUITE GOOD AT THIS
but it's not the best use of your time.

START HERE!

YOU FIND YOURSELF DOING THIS
but don't want to spend your time here.

YOU DREAD DOING THESE TASKS
& they've got to go.

CREATE A PLAN to hand off the bottom sections as soon as possible. Look for repeatable activities in the top boxes, as those are also great to delegate! Run this exercise periodically to increase the delegation.

The four corners where our time lives.

Step 1: In the box that follows, which duplicates the top left corner of the Delegate Freedom Analysis graphic, write your answers to the question: *"What are the things that I want to be spending my time on?"* These should be positive things tied to your most impactful contribution and your goals. Refer back to your earlier work in Chapter 1.

For example, you may want to spend time on:

1. Key relationships

2. Big ideas

3. Strategy

4. Writing

5. Being a guest on podcasts

Your Turn

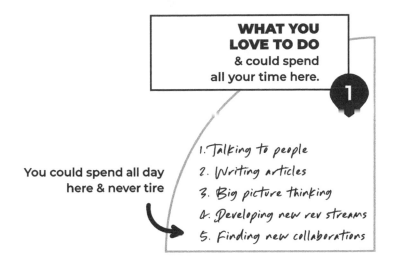

WHAT YOU LOVE TO DO & could spend all your time here.

1

You could spend all day here & never tire

1. Talking to people
2. Writing articles
3. Big picture thinking
4. Developing new rev streams
5. Finding new collaborations

List the things that you want to spend your time on.

Now list three adjectives from the earlier chapters that describe how spending time doing these things will make you feel:

1. _____

2. _____

3. _____

Step 2: Let's move to the bottom right corner of the Delegate Freedom Analysis graphic and capture everything you're doing that sucks your time and energy. You despise this work, but it's still on your plate. In the next box below, list the tasks that you want off your plate along with how much time they take each week, and who might be able to do those things instead.

For example:

1. Scheduling: five hours/week, Mary

2. Replying to emails: ten hours/week, Carlos

3. Organizing my Dropbox: one hour/week, Amanda

4. Paying bills: one hour/week, Chris

Your Turn

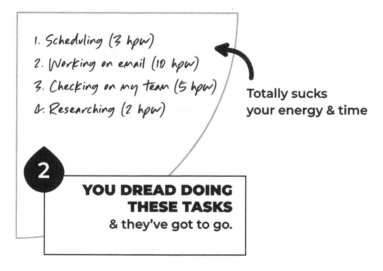

1. Scheduling (3 hpw)
2. Working on email (10 hpw)
3. Checking on my team (5 hpw)
4. Researching (2 hpw)

**Totally sucks
your energy & time**

2

**YOU DREAD DOING
THESE TASKS**
& they've got to go.

*List the tasks that you want off your plate, how much time
they take per week, and who will do them.*

Everything you list here is going to be the first to go. Once you clear those things off, that newly found time and energy should be immediately redirected and refilled by the top left corner activities.

How many hours each week will you be saving now?

I'm spending _____ hours each week doing work that totally sucks my energy and time.

Capture three adjectives that describe how spending your time on these activities makes you feel:

1. _____

2. _____

3. _____

Look back at step one and compare these adjectives. This should motivate you to keep working through this process to get you further elevated. Stay with the emotions as we continue on!

Bonus points for this section and next. Ask yourself, *"What are things that I am doing more than once?"* These repeatable activities are some of the best delegation candidates because you can create a simple process around them and hand them off to an *assistant.* As you are working on this, jot some names down next to each activity and think about *who* could take this task over for you.

And, remember, if you don't have an assistant, you ARE the assistant!

Step 3: Now, shift to the bottom left corner of the Delegate Freedom Analysis graphic. In the box that follows, list the things that you find yourself spending your time on but don't like doing. Sometimes it's a nice mind-numbing opportunity to escape the more challenging parts of your day to do some simple tasks. Note how much time the task takes each week, and who could potentially take it over for you.

For example:

1. Sending contracts: one hour/week, Beth

2. Lead follow-up/nurture: two hours/week, Mackenzie

3. Creating processes: one hour/week, Georgia

4. Setting up systems: one hour/week, Eric

5. Keeping things moving and on track: three hours/week, Stella

Your Turn

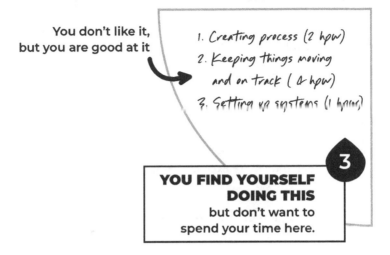

You don't like it, but you are good at it

1. Creating process (2 hpw)
2. Keeping things moving and on track (4 hpw)
3. Setting up systems (1 hour)

YOU FIND YOURSELF DOING THIS but don't want to spend your time here.

3

List the tasks you don't like doing, how much time they take per week, and who might do them.

How many hours will you be reclaiming each week?

I'm spending _____ hours each week doing work that I don't like that someone else could do as well as if not better than me.

Step 4: Now we move to the last and final portion of this exercise, the top right corner of the Delegate Freedom Analysis graphic. It's the hardest box to tackle because typically we are quite good at these things and enjoy them, which is why we spend a lot of time doing them. But they are not the best use of our time and get in the way of quality time we can spend on our most impactful contribution. This can be really hard work, because we have to go deep within ourselves and stay connected to what we are here to do, instead of what feels most comfortable to us.

With that in mind, let's dig deep and move to the upper right corner of our exercise.

What to look for here:

- You like it and you're excellent at it.

- You're doing it more than once.

- Others can potentially do it as well as you.

For example, one big activity that I was able to move off my plate in this area was launching new clients. I was great at helping create a delegation strategy. I liked extending a warm welcome to our new clients, getting to know them, and introducing my team. However, it also took a lot of my time each week to prep for the call, run the call, and do follow-up after the call.

Yet the more I thought about it, the more I began to realize it was a repeatable thing that I was doing, which had a process, even though it currently lived in my head. This meant that I could simply work with one of my team members to document the process, train, shadow, and then hand it over.

This was not a simple realization, because I took a lot of pride in this part of my contribution. I was worried about whether clients would get the same experience with someone else on my team running these calls.

But we persisted. We worked tirelessly together to capture the process so that one of my team members could take over. She shadowed me, I shadowed her, and then she was off and running. This handoff freed up at least five hours per week for me, and empowered one of my team members to do more meaningful work.

Once we created the process, we were able to build out a small team of "client launchers" that now run all of our client kickoffs. Because they are so attuned to the service delivery, they have evolved it, perfected it, and made it better than when I was running it. So, I encourage you to go really deep here. The things you capture in the following box are things that you may hold near and dear as part of your role. Likely they bring you confidence and satisfaction of a job well done, but they're not the highest and best use of your time! They're not moving your vision forward, nor are they your most impactful contribution.

Okay, deep breaths. Let's start with a few examples:

1. Business development/sales calls

2. Writing marketing content

3. Working conference booths

4. Launching new clients

Your Turn

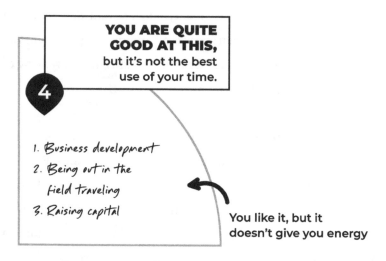

YOU ARE QUITE GOOD AT THIS, but it's not the best use of your time.

4

1. Business development
2. Being out in the field traveling
3. Raising capital

You like it, but it doesn't give you energy

Things you are excellent at and enjoy, but get in the way of time spent on your most impactful contribution.

How many hours will you be saving each week?

I'm spending _____ hours doing work that I like and I'm good at, but it isn't my most impactful contribution.

Your Total Hours to Delegate

First, look back at steps two, three, and four above and calculate how many total hours you are spending each week outside your most impactful contribution: _____

Now, look back at Chapter 2, step two, to the section on Understanding Your Worth and write your hourly rate here: $_____.

Next, multiply the number of hours you're spending doing work outside your most impactful contribution each week and multiply it by your hourly rate:

- Example: 25 hours/week × $120/hour = $3,000 per week

- Your turn: _____ hours/week × $_____/hour = $_____ per week

Finally, take that number and make it annual by multiplying it by fifty-two weeks:

- Example: $3,000 per week × 52 weeks = $156,000

- Your turn: $_____ per week × 52 weeks = $_____

This is how much you are paying yourself each year to do work that is outside your most impactful contribution.

Repeat this out loud: I'm spending $_____ annually, paying myself to do work that someone else could do better than me, instead of putting that time and energy into (insert answers from step one) _____.

That sentence alone should be a jolt to your mindset around the cost of *not* delegating well. In our example and in workshops I've given on this content, I've seen that number go as high as six figures. Six figures! We are paying ourselves six figures to do work we don't like, aren't great at, and that isn't moving our most impactful contribution forward.

Write down three adjectives for how this exercise makes you feel.

1. _____

2. _____

3. _____

Take Action

1. Circle the bottom part of the exercise. That's what you are targeting first.

2. Next to each of the tasks for which you have jotted down names of team members, schedule some time to talk with each person about taking these things off your plate.

3. If you don't have names listed because you don't have anyone in place to take these things over, it's time to hire.

Force yourself to look at the figure you are paying yourself each year to do work that is outside your most impactful contribution. It will inspire you to take action. Even hiring a fractional executive assistant will cost you a small amount in comparison to the work you're doing that is not the highest and best use of your time.

4. Commit to solve, but baby step your way through this. We will cover many of the best practices to actually delegate these things in the next chapter, but don't just dump and run. It is bound to blow up in your face, and you will find yourself back where you started.

RECAP

Let's recap and build on some of the essentials we've covered in the book so far.

Repeat your affirmation. My affirmation that I will repeat to myself when I start to feel negatively about letting go of tasks is:

_____

The impact I will make by doing these things (my why) is:

_____

Not delegating tasks is costing me: _____ annually. I will reference this data point as I make decisions around what is coming off my plate and ask myself if the tasks that I am doing are that dollar value.

You now have your vision for your time solidly in place. You know what you want to spend your time on. You know what's got to go. Next, we will look at how to effectively move tasks off your plate using the science of delegation.

CHAPTER 6

THE SCIENCE

"Everything is theoretically impossible,
until it's done."

—ROBERT A. HEINLEIN

S o far in Part 2, we've taken a deep dive into the discipline of
delegation, the challenges of why we struggle with delegation,
and how to overcome these challenges. We explored the art of delegation, and you created a working list of what you can hand off to
your team. In this chapter, we'll explore the science of delegation,
which is the primary technical component of how delegation is
done well.

Imagine this component as the last ingredient of a great cake. For
the cake to rise and be fabulous, it needs baking soda. It's an ordi-
nary ingredient, but it's also what makes the cake a success. The

cake might be filled with lots of great artistic ingredients like flour, sugar, eggs, nuts, and chocolate, but if we forget to add the baking soda, the cake is flat and disappointing. The same is true with our delegation practice. Being able to execute our handoff well is the mainstay ingredient that must always be present for our final delegation recipe to be a success. We begin studying the science of delegation with a few golden rules.

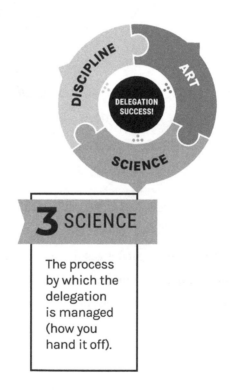

The science of delegation is the primary technical component of delegating well.

THE FIVE GOLDEN RULES
OF SUCCESSFUL DELEGATION™

I recommend five best practices for how to successfully hand off tasks. After we run through these key concepts, I'll present examples of the principles applied in real-life scenarios.

1. Always Delegate the End Result

Paint the picture of what success looks like when the project or task is done. By sharing this, you let team members find their own way. You may be surprised, they just might do it better and faster than you could, but you will end up with the overall result you wanted in the end. Share these thoughts with your support partners and explain what has to be true when it's completed, and let them take it from there. Encourage their questions so they feel comfortable and confident with their next steps.

Bonus points here for sharing why the project is important to you and for achieving the end result.

2. Feedback Is a Must

Delegation is not a singular experience, even at the task level. The commitment to give and receive feedback helps you become a stronger delegator and helps bring your delegatee more in sync with a shared goal.

If the person to whom you delegate tasks does well, share why it was helpful. This will help them view their work in connection to the bigger picture. Let them give you feedback as well, so you can become a stronger delegator.

3. Start Small to Build Confidence

Focus on compartmentalizing larger tasks and projects into smaller pieces to build your own confidence around delegation. This strategy takes the fear and overwhelm away from something that might feel too big or scary to let go of.

Remember to always start with repeatables and low-hanging fruit delegations. Grab the small wins! It still equates to time saved, and you'll build confidence in this phase.

4. Get Comfortable with 80 Percent

Remember, we are going for progress not perfection. Ask yourself, *"If someone can do this 80 percent as well as I could, will that be good enough?"* Take the time to work through the success details and share your *why* to help increase this percentage.

You can also think about the 80/20 rule in relation to having someone do 80 percent of the work, leaving you with the remaining 20 percent—the final tweaks and special touches.

And sometimes, having someone just *start* something for you is a win! I use this strategy all the time because it reduces the overall pressure on me to see it through so we can collectively check it off.

5. Commit to the Boring Stuff

The boring stuff makes up at least 50 percent of your business and it is important! The back office boring stuff is the backbone of how you deliver what you do in an effective, unique way and creates scale. Ignoring it because it's either not interesting or not a competence for you is not serving your vision.

The beauty about delegation is that you're not charged with doing it or hammering out the details to bring it to life. However, you must be able to articulate your operational vision well to your team. Understand that your ongoing commitment to seeing the process of delegation through is critical, and that it may take many iterations of an administrative process to find the right solution.

Of these five golden rules, which one do you feel you've already mastered or do well, and why?

Which one(s) feel harder or more challenging to you and why?

GOLDEN RULES IN
REAL LIFE

Let's break these best golden rule practices down to a real-life example and template that you can follow. We'll use the number one activity everyone should be delegating: scheduling.

Follow this simple template to hand off with ease:

1. Describe what success looks like to hand off your scheduling work and why it's important. Remember, always delegate the end result.

   Scheduling Example:

   a. In order for my scheduling to be successfully handed off, the following must be true:

      i. Meeting confirmations are happening one day prior to avoid last-minute cancellations.

      ii. Scheduling conversations are responded to twice per day.

      iii. We always offer at least three slots when possible.

iv. We always include our time zone (ET) when we send options.

v. I have a fifteen-minute buffer time between each meeting.

vi. I have at least a half hour for lunch midday.

vii. We are grouping similar meetings together whenever possible.

viii. Travel time is calculated as buffer time between meetings.

ix. Naming conventions are set and followed whenever we send the invite.

x. And so on... continue to capture here what must be true for you to feel comfortable.

b. Why this project is important to me:

i. Because my time is my most valuable asset.

ii. I want to work as strategically as possible and manage my energy across the day.

iii. Properly delegating helps me make my best impact.

iv. It also allows me to be present for my friends and family.

v. It keeps me from having to manage these details.

Your Turn

Pick a big delegation and describe what success looks like for this project when completed and why it's important to you:

_____

_____

_____

2. Activate the handoff. Once you've identified and aligned on what success looks like around your project or task, it's time to prepare to hand off.

   Scheduling Example:

   a. Meet with your support partner and have them review the success list above in advance of your meeting. They may bring questions, so encourage that.

   b. Answer any questions and establish next best steps.

      i. Discuss tech access. How are they accessing your calendar? Do they need a dedicated email or will they be responding as you? We suggest a mix of both.

      ii. Set up the parameters of your calendar. Your ideal start and end times. Make sure you schedule in your free time, add vacations, ideal days off, etc.

iii. Work to streamline your calendar into something that matches your energy shifts. For me, I load my week with meetings on Monday and Tuesday, leave Wednesday to clean up to-dos, and spend Thursday writing. Friday is a free day for me to work on whatever is pressing or interesting and I shut down early. I add my workout blocks on Monday and Wednesday mornings and don't start my day with any calls before 10 a.m. Think through what works best for you.

iv. Review anything currently on your calendar that doesn't need to be there, such as recurring internal meetings you've "always" been part of but likely don't need to attend. Just have your assistant request a recap of that meeting and have them share any headlines with you in a systematic, easy way until you feel comfortable and have the proper accountability in place with your absence.

v. Time blocking is my favorite part of ensuring an effective week. Work with your scheduling partner to perfect your time blocking. In your weekly meeting, look ahead each week and think through any prep slots you might need. Grab them and have your support partner add any attachments or points of reference so you don't need to dig around to find the info. You could set a standing block, such as bill paying. You can build up things across the week that need to happen during that block and just reference it when you are in the block. *Bonus points: Have your assistant add things to that time block for you to review as they see them come through and learn more about what's urgent versus what's important.*

c. Last, establish a cadence to check in and set expectations on how you want to communicate. For example: "Let's meet on Mondays and Wednesdays for thirty minutes each week until you feel comfortable. I can answer questions for you and we can talk through any challenges or modifications we need to make." Encourage them to bring feedback to this meeting for you as well, regarding what's working versus what's not, and make this a healthy and regular part of your conversations.

Bonus points: Can you identify possible ways to use automation in your scheduling? For example, perhaps you can use a scheduling link for internal meetings to save everyone time.

Your Turn

Fill this in during your handoff meeting.

The next best steps we will take are:

_____

_____

_____

We've established the following communication cadence to check in on this delegation:

_____

3. Set success metrics and establish ownership and accountability. The last step to complete your successful handoff is about transfer of ownership.

    Scheduling Example:

    a. Agree together that your support partner ultimately owns your calendar. This is important because it keeps you from interfering as much as possible and offering competing times to what they may have already offered someone else. Agree on what *you* can add and how you will communicate.

    b. Brainstorm a few metrics for success tied to things that are important to you. It could be reflective. For example: you were able to spend X percent of your week doing one key activity because of diligent scheduling. It could be that you took X number of free days because your support partner protected your time. It could also be predictive, like X number of sales calls scheduled. Set them and integrate them into your weekly or biweekly check-in conversation and agenda.

c. Establish what will happen if these metrics go off track and commit to always discuss them together and adjust for the future.

Your Turn

Establish who is doing what and by when, and when you will meet next to check in. Can you identify any metrics that might indicate the delegation is going off track?

_____

_____

_____

Remember, your ability to "rock the handoff" is your path to finding more freedom. Having a reliable delegation partner who understands where you are trying to go and why, and is then equipped with what they need to effectively take it off your plate, is your ticket out and up into the elevation stratosphere.

RECAP

Let's recap and build on some of the essentials we've covered so far.

1. I commit to responsibly hand off the following task/project:

   _____

2. My most impactful contribution is: _____

   _____

3. The impact I will make by spending my time doing these things (my why) is: _____

   _____

4. Not doing this well is costing me: $_____ in time and energy each year.

5. My affirmation that I will repeat to myself when I start to feel negatively about letting go is: _____

   _____

Next, in Part 3 of the book, it all comes together in the execution, as we take a closer look at a delegation system you can use to reliably delegate on repeat.

PART 3

EXECUTION

*"Average people have great ideas.
Legends have great execution."*

—Anonymous

CHAPTER 7

RELIABLE AND REPEATABLE DELEGATION

"Give a man a fish and you feed him for a day;
teach a man to fish and you
feed him for a lifetime."

—CHINESE PROVERB

The challenge I see many leaders face when it comes to implementing delegation in a repeatable, reliable way is that there is no clear system that is easy to follow. Without some level of organization, these "random acts of delegation" just confuse our teams, create chaos, and are usually not handled thoughtfully enough to ensure success or impact. Implementing a delegation system in your business ensures that everyone is thinking about delegation in the same meaningful, effective way. With the deep knowledge you now have around how and what to delegate, I'm going to introduce a simple delegation system you can easily follow to make delegation part of your daily routine, so you can finally let go.

Sometimes, in the chaos of our days, it's easy to try to create space by randomly dumping tasks on people, or throwing up our hands in frustration, or dropping balls because we are simply overwhelmed. A simple delegation system provides us with a format, structure, and clear set of guidelines that we can build on when our time starts to get away from us.

THE DELEGATE FREEDOM SYSTEM™

With so much delegation content and training out there, why do we still struggle with it? Now that we've addressed the mindset and the tactical side of delegation, we are going to focus on execution. In my years running a delegation company, I've found that there was no precise system for delegation, so I created one!

Using what we know must be true for delegation to work well, even when things get crazy and we are in the thick of it, a simple system provides us with an effective way to think about delegation. I developed the five-step Delegate Freedom System™ as a method we can cling to in a reliable and repeatable way, allowing leaders to operationalize delegation for themselves and their teams.

The five-step Delegate Freedom System™ is simple, reliable, and repeatable.

The Delegate Freedom System™ is designed to run as a circular system that repeats with ease. This holistic approach combines all of our earlier learning and makes your elevated day possible. A cyclical five-step process allows you to focus on impactful and energizing work while ensuring that lower-ROI tasks can be successfully cleared from your plate.

Remember, delegation is not meant to be a singular experience. It is continuous and ongoing. This process can be part of your daily or weekly routine, no matter to whom you're delegating. And, as you start to shift your mindset from delegation being a chore to using it as a tool to manage your energy, you will find yourself doing more and more of it. Hence the need for a reliable, simple system to follow to increase your chances of doing it well and finding success.

As we explore this system, keep in mind that a great assistant can help prompt you through this process in a weekly meeting. Now how's that for delegation?

Step 1: Focus

The system begins by focusing on your most impactful contribution. Remember our work on mindset from Part 1 of the book? It applies here as well. Center yourself to get clear on how you want to spend your time and energy. Create a vision for your time, where most of it is spent doing your most impactful work.

This part of the process is meant to prepare you for a successful handoff. Do not skip this step. While all steps of the process are equally important, this first step tends to be glossed over because it's tied to your mindset and vision for yourself. This is the vital step where you get clarity and reconnect with how you really want to spend your time. It's crucial to keep in touch with yourself as you work the delegation system.

Parkinson's Law again applies here: "Work expands to fill the time available for it." Because time is like a vacuum, if you do not have clarity around how you actually want to spend your time, all kinds of energy vampires will creep in to fill it back up as you try to let go. To combat that, you must have a vision for and limits on your time that you can clearly see, or you will find yourself back in the busyness of your day.

Clarity at this phase makes the rest of the process a breeze because you've invested intentionally early on. This is also the opportunity to mentally prepare yourself for delegation by reciting an affirmation or two to build your confidence. Give yourself permission to create boundaries that are tied to your goals and values. *Remember, if you don't own your time, someone else does!*

A quick note about time blocking: we have numerous reference materials about the power of time blocking and how to do it on our website at <u>letitgodelegationbook.com</u>. I could write an entire chapter about how to use it effectively to get what you want from your week. But the concept is simple: intentionally design how you want to spend your time. Mark the boxes of time on your calendar and follow them each week. Map the placement of them to your energy and your priorities in set units of time. The stricter you are with the time you give to each task, the more focused and results-driven your work output will be as you're pressed to move to the next block of time. In fact, following time blocking was the only way I was able to get this book written and turned in on time!

Getting Focused

1. Set a time block for yourself to quietly reflect with consistency. It can be daily or weekly, but it is a sacred, recurring time. For me, it's Monday mornings after my meditation, smoothie, and workout so that I start my week off with a clear head and vision for my time.

2. Revisit your most impactful contribution, and ask yourself, *"What do I want to spend my time on this week?"* Be selfish!

   a. Write down your most impactful contribution. My most impactful contribution is: _____

   _____

   b. State your why. The impact I will make by spending my time doing these things (my why) is:

   _____

   c. I want to spend my time this week doing:

   _____

3. Look at your week ahead and make sure you have set time aside to actually spend on those things. Claim the time before other people do!

4. Revisit your affirmation so that you have a clear mind and heart going into the next step.

a. Repeat your affirmation. My affirmation that I will repeat to myself when I start to shift to a negative headspace about letting go is:

_____

I recommend doing this step weekly, if not daily, especially in the beginning. I tend to do this on Monday mornings, before I start any meetings, to better prepare for my week. The goal here is to have total clarity on what you *want* to spend your time on and intentionally structure your time to make that happen. But stay true to your energy patterns. If you're most productive at a certain time of day, or day of the week, capitalize on that energy to get the most out of this step.

Your Turn

- Start with positive past wins. Is there a habit, mindset, or practice you've implemented for yourself that helped you be more focused? _____

  ▷ What was it? _____

  ▷ Why do you think it helped you? _____

- When do you think is the best time of week or day to work on the first step? _____

- Now, schedule it in!

Step 2: Evaluate

After you've gotten back in touch with your focus for the day or week through reflection and affirmation in step one, review your calendar and objectively *evaluate* how your time is spent and if it's advancing your goals. Think about who can take on work you don't like or aren't good at.

Step two is about learning! You want to systematically evaluate the reality of how your time is currently being spent to see what you can learn. We start first with a review of the past and work through to the present. This is a great chance to reintroduce the Freedom Analysis™ exercise from Chapter 5 on the art of delegation. In step two of the delegation system, you are on a fact-finding mission to objectively review your ideal day and week versus the reality of how it plays out now.

Ask yourself:

- What trends do you see?

- What are you doing more than once?

- What do you really want to spend your time on once you are better leveraged?

- How will being able to do that make you feel?

- Are there any tasks or projects you need to handle that can be grouped together and handled in a time block to maintain focus and energy?

Because you took the time in step one to get clarity on how you want to spend your time, you'll start to see the impact of your time and energy being wasted on lower-value work. Many of our clients have us run reports and calculate how they spent their time based on what's on their calendar. We then score it and study the data together and use it to create rules and even more boundaries to better protect their time.

You can also use this step to objectively track progress by attributing dollars to how your time is spent. Over time, you'll watch it shift week over week as you let go of more and more. This is also an opportunity to think about *who* can take on a lot of the work you don't like or aren't good at. So, as you write your list, note who you can potentially hand each task and activity to. Be hyperaware and sensitive to work you've done or are scheduled to do that doesn't energize you.

Execution of This Step Daily or Weekly

1. Past: Look at last week and reflect, what did you spend your time on?

   a. What things did you do that you could have delegated?

b. Write those things down and review them with your support partner in your next meeting and brainstorm together.

c. Consider adding initials next to each item as you think about who could have handled that instead of you.

d. Did you try any time blocking and how did that go?

e. Score the last week from one to ten. How did you do with delegating and spending time on your most impactful contribution?

2. Future: Now, write down your priorities for this week— your "must accomplish" list.

a. Ensure you are spending at least some of your time on your why, your most impactful contribution.

b. Make sure you have added time blocks for that, as well as your other priorities for the week.

c. Are there any parts on your "must accomplish" list that you could delegate to someone else, even if it's merely a portion? Write those things down and write their initials next to them.

3. Present: Take one last look at your to-do list that might have carried over from last week.

a. What things still need to get done?

b. What things on that list can someone else do for you? Add their initials.

c. If you need a time block to get those things done, add it now.

4. Last step: Look at your calendar and notice any trends that you might see.

a. Is there a call that can be moved on Friday so that you can take the day off?

b. Is there a way to streamline certain types of meetings together?

c. Do you need to add or modify any time blocks?

d. Can some of your calls be moved so that you can get a good time block in?

Bonus 1: Have your assistant map your ideal week overlaid against your actual week. You'll see very clearly how your time is being spent versus how you want to spend it, and you can make adjustments.

Bonus 2: Capture your personal priorities as well.

Bonus 3: Continue to ideate on rules for your calendar to create some additional freedom in how you're spending your day. This level of iteration will help you dial into the most perfect ideal week.

Bonus 4: Don't forget about your energy! Reflect on what other changes you want to make on your calendar to account for how you felt last week. Example: Do you need a time block after certain meetings to handle or hand off possible to-dos? Note that change here and add your support partner's initials to discuss in your next meeting.

Your Turn

- What trends do you see?

  _____

- What are you doing more than once?

  _____

- What do you really want to spend your time on once you are better leveraged?

  _____

- How will being able to do that make you feel?

  _____

- What are some new time blocks you can add to minimize distractions?

Step 3: Prioritize

Create a delegation strategy that's tied to your goals and priorities to ensure that what's being handed off truly moves the needle to get you closer to your elevated day.

This is the step most people race through when they begin delegating, especially entrepreneurs who tend to have shiny object syndrome when it comes to maintaining their attention. This behavior is another reason why they feel delegation never works for them, because they keep jumping from priority to priority, confusing themselves and their teams and never really gaining momentum.

In our work with clients, we always start with a customized delegation strategy that is tied to their goals and priorities to keep things on track. Without this, delegation falls flat because it's running rampant without a clear leverage plan. When you take the time to have clarity on your most impactful contribution, *and* you couple that with clarity around the goals you are chasing and have committed to, you are starting delegation with a really solid foundation that will finally make an impact.

Delegation should always start from your established goals. The ability to have leverage aligned with your focus should always be part of your initial strategy when you look at what to delegate. From there, once those goals-focused delegations are captured and prioritized, *then* you can start to look at the low-hanging fruit, the work you don't like to do and aren't good at.

Execution of Step 3

Execution of this step can be done daily or weekly.

1. Write down your goals for the quarter, month, and year.

2. Think through what *you* specifically need to do to make those things happen.

3. Brainstorm some of the other associated to-dos that might help you get that goal to "done." You may find that your only contribution is 10 to 20 percent of the overall project. This is a great step to brainstorm with a support partner who has a strong capability with taking a big picture and breaking it down into small next steps.

4. Be realistic here. There are bound to be additional to-dos and low-hanging fruit activities that are on your plate that must also get handled.

    a. Begin to prompt yourself as you capture those with,

"Do I really need to do that? Who can do that instead of me?"

b. Write down any to-dos that are outside of your goals and priorities, and add any initials to to-dos that you can possibly hand off.

c. Don't forget any personal things; it's one big pot of time after all.

Your Turn

1. My goals and priorities for this month, quarter, or year are:

▷ _____ _____

▷ _____

▷ _____

2. When it comes to my goals and priorities for this month or quarter, the pieces that *only* I can do are:

_____

(the rest of getting this done needs to be delegated).

3. My team can help me accomplish these goals and priorities by handling:

▷ _____

▷ _____

▷ _____

4. The other things that I must get done this week are:

▷ _____

▷ _____

▷ _____

Step 4: Handoff

As part of the handoff, clearly describe what success looks like, establish metrics for it, and sync on who is doing what and by when.

Getting this step right helps you ensure success, which is what will build your confidence with delegation. Now that you've figured out *what* to delegate, you still have to rock the actual handoff to the person you are delegating to. *Be sure to refer back to Chapter 6 and follow The Five Golden Rules of Successful Delegation™.*

The key to a successful handoff is to first have clarity. Sometimes we get so excited about a new project or idea that we don't take the time or don't have the interest to really think it through before we set it in motion. When we rush through this step, we create messes and endlessly confuse our teams.

This is the step where you flesh out your delegation ideas in detail, and make sure they are actually important to you. It also helps you to describe what success looks like to your support partner. This tells them what needs to be true when the project is complete, but allows them to get to the same result in a way that works for them. And who knows, maybe it's a better way than you've considered!

If what you're trying to delegate is a process, let them interview you, or have them watch you perform the process, while they capture notes. Again, our goal is to get any repeatables that you are doing yourself out of your head and into a process that can be handed off. Anything you are doing more than once is a candidate for delegation!

Be sure to end this handoff step by selecting some simple metrics that will objectively confirm if the delegation is on track or off track.

One important thing to note that makes for a really solid handoff: "If nobody owns it, it never gets done." Or, the inverse of that: "When nobody owns it, messes happen." What this means is that sometimes our tendency is to hand off and check out. But, if we relinquish ownership of getting the thing across the finish line, meaning the whole thing done, we need to effectively transfer the ownership of that finish line to someone else.

For example, a few years back I decided that I would like to offer a scholarship program to support a company that was making an impact in my community, and that could be even more impactful if they were better leveraged administratively. I shared the idea, got my leadership team on board with it quickly, and launched it.

Each of us owned different pieces that were overall quite successful (promoting the program, paying for it, working with our team to select the client, and then working with the client). Unfortunately, no one owned the overall scope of the project from start to finish (*and therefore I owned it because it was my idea*). So as the months went on, the scholarship recipient was supported and achieved great success, but no one on my team was thinking about a plan to close things out and take maximum advantage of this great opportunity to share about our work in a meaningful way. We had all done our collective pieces, but at the end, we had shifted our focus to other new pressing projects. I found myself rushing, realizing I needed to coordinate a case study and social media campaign when we were done, because no one owned the entire project from start to finish, and I had stopped thinking about it months prior when my initial piece was done. While the program was a great success and we did help a great cause, we didn't take full, thoughtful advantage of sharing the overall impact of our work, because I was already on to newer projects and hadn't delegated the success of the entire program to someone.

It's really easy to start to delegate pieces of projects, and I whole-heartedly encourage it! But keep in mind that assigning an owner for an entire project to see things through from ideation to completion is part of a successful handoff, particularly if it's something meaty and large. Otherwise, it will be you!

Execution of Step 4

1. Your goal is to get as much as possible off your plate responsibly. Look over what you have listed in your goals and priorities earlier in step three of the delegation system.

   a. Are any of the smaller items listed there repeatables? If so, you need a time block to run someone through your process. Don't forget to have them capture it for future purposes!

2. For any of the larger delegations, follow these steps:

   a. Confirm that it's still important to you and a delegation priority for the week.

      i. If not, drop it down to a parking lot for later.

      ii. Add some context for yourself around *when* it needs to be completed and note that next to it.

      iii. Flesh out what success looks like before you hand it off to that person to complete the task.

      iv. Consider adding a success metric to objectively confirm it's on track for completion.

    v. Agree on who owns seeing this through from start
       to finish.

   vi. Start with explaining *why* this is important to you.
       Give some context as to the big picture and how
       this particular thing fits in.

  vii. Then share what has to be true when the delegation
       is complete and agree on turnaround time
       expectations.

Your Turn

1. My goals and priorities for this week, month, quarter, or
   year are: _____
   and are important to me because _____
   _____.

2. I will see delegation of this project/task as a success, as
   long as these things are true:

   a. _____

   b. _____

   c. _____

   d. _____

   e. _____

3. _____ (Name) is doing _____
_____ (What) by _____
(When).

Step 5: Feedback

Establish a healthy and open feedback loop by setting expectations and guidelines around regular ongoing evaluations of what's working and what's not.

Think of this step as a mini wheel spinning endlessly around as many of your delegations as possible, especially early on. To build confidence, we need our delegations to work, and we need to feel the impact. If any part of this early experience breaks and we don't address it, the frustration will build, and we will once again throw up our hands and say we're not good delegators.

So, stop the madness and form a healthy feedback loop from the beginning to remain in an energized place with delegation. What worked? What didn't work? What can we learn from this to do better in the future? Commit to this process with every delegation early on, or in every weekly meeting you have with your support team thereafter. We can learn so much from the breakdowns.

When you start to delegate to someone, set some guidelines in the beginning that promote the spirit of ongoing, iterative feedback on what's working and what's not, and that if something breaks, it's not personal. Establish that this will be a healthy rhythm between you and your delegation partner that you commit to do consistently so nothing builds up. Ask *them* what you can do better to make the delegations flow more smoothly, and be receptive to feedback. In this way, you lead by example. If it breaks, and it's bad, stop what you're doing, meet, and complete the feedback loop in the moment, or as soon as possible while it's fresh. Grab the learnings and apply them to the future. If nothing breaks in a given week, still meet to discuss and celebrate the wins, take the learnings, and update any processes to reflect what worked. And remember, you're dealing with other humans, and mistakes *will* happen. The key is to find the learning to be better for next time.

Execution of Step 5

1. Establish a communication cadence around the delegation.

    a. For each delegation that is more complex, or for each delegation where you don't have a standing meeting with that person each week, commit to a consistent way to pulse while they are working on what was delegated to them.

    b. For those that you delegate to regularly, incorporate this step into your weekly agenda. The concept is simply what's working and what's not working.

You can add this into the agenda after you sync on where things are with various delegations.

c. Empower your team to own/run that meeting. *Not* you. Your job is to answer questions and give feedback.

2. Consider whether you need to account for a time block for yourself within this process to finalize the overall task/project. Add it to your calendar.

3. Commit to the pulsing schedule. Add it to your calendar as a recurring time block.

4. See if you can identify any success metrics or leading indicators of success or failure with a key delegation to indicate possible breakdowns.

a. *Example: We have 500 rows of data to organize by Friday. Today is Tuesday, so that means we need to get through 125 rows per day. Does that seem doable? Why not try today and see how long it takes you per row and let's make sure we can hit that goal, in case we need to bring in more people to help.*

The more you can start to predict and anticipate breakdowns and plan for them, the greater confidence you will have when delegating. Now that you have a system that you can operationalize to better protect your time and energy, let's look at how we can use it and the other concepts presented in earlier chapters to truly elevate yourself.

Your Turn

- _____ (Name) and I will pulse at _____ frequency to check in and feedback, and it's on both of our calendars ☐ Y / ☐ N.

- _____ (Name) will run the meeting, not me.

- We've identified a leading indicator/success metric of _____ that will give us advance notice if the delegation is getting off track.

Repeat your affirmation. My affirmation that I will repeat to myself when I start to feel negatively about letting go is:

_____

I commit to use the Delegate Freedom System™ to hand off the following task/project:

_____

CHAPTER 8

THE TEN HABITS AND MINDSETS OF ELEVATED LEADERS

"You can't talk butterfly language with caterpillar people."

—Anonymous

Let's return to Tom and his delegation story from Part 1. When we left off, Tom was deeply conflicted about letting go of his "busy work" for reasons that had absolutely nothing to do with his assistant Anne or her ability to help him. After the loss of his father, Tom had to quickly figure out what his own most impactful contribution was going to be to the company he inherited. Rather than living out his father's legacy, he knew he wanted to build from what his father had done, and create his own path.

After a month or so of running his company without his dad, Tom was feeling burnt out, frustrated, and lost. Mostly, he was mad at himself for not investing time in himself to feel clear of his own vision for the company. Tom took a long weekend up at his family's cabin by himself to really get in touch with his emotions and perception of what he wanted to contribute. He left that trip with a newfound fire, passion, and life purpose. A former college athlete, Tom discovered that his own personal mission was to build an award-winning culture, to create a company filled with great people doing great work that they were excited about. His most impactful contribution was to coach, empower, and encourage his team to do their best work. He thought that if he had happy employees doing work they loved, they were bound to be even more successful.

Taking this on meant there would need to be a massive shift in the existing culture at his company. His father's era of ownership, while profitable and effective, had created an old regime of folks who were hardworking, nice people, but were not totally a true culture fit for his vision. Tom knew that for him to live out his purpose, he had to quickly shift most of his day-to-day work over to Anne and the rest of his management team. He had to learn how to elevate his time, and delegate more quickly.

Elevating your time is a lot like going to the gym to build muscle. It takes time, commitment, and a little pain to sculpt a muscle. Elevated leaders consistently execute on a mix of five habits and five mindsets to find new ways to free up their time. Because acknowledging progress can create confidence and momentum along your delegation journey, I've created a "scorecard" that you can use to measure yourself as you look to improve your delegation practice. As you develop more mastery, you can come back to rescore yourself and feel your progress. You can access the full scorecard via our website at letitgodelegationbook.com. ⓘ

THE FIVE HABITS

Let's start by looking at the habits that must exist for us to find true leverage. A habit is a behavior that starts as a choice, and then becomes a nearly unconscious pattern. In each of the following habits, score yourself based on where you are *now* with each.

Instructions: Under each section, score yourself on a scale of one to ten based on the statement that most aligns with where you are today. You can revisit this exercise over time to track your improvements! A ten is perfect and near impossible—it's the ideal—the horizon we are chasing as we get better and better.

1. My Vision

This habit is where it all begins. Our ability to identify, connect with, and take action on our vision is what makes us successful and impactful leaders. This means that you have a crystal-clear vision on what you're here to do, what your contribution should be, and how you want to spend your time. Highly visioned leaders can articulate their vision to their teams effectively and leverage them to move their vision forward. Their ability to document the vision and the next best steps with success metrics keeps the team aligned and rowing together in the same direction.

Score Yourself: _____

10	9 8 7	6 5 4	3 2 1
I have a crystal-clear vision on what I'm here to do, what my contribution should be, and how to spend my time. I can easily articulate it, and it's documented so that my team also knows how to support my efforts.	I have a good picture of what I'm here to do, what my contribution should be, and how I should spend my time. I have articulated my vision to my team, but I'm still being pulled into work that isn't tied to my vision.	I struggle with fully understanding my vision and being able to articulate it. I haven't written it down or devoted energy to thinking about or trying to solve it, which is making my team unclear on how they can help.	I'm unclear about what I should be spending my time on and what my contribution really is. I tend to spend my days putting out fires and cleaning up messes and find myself constantly busy with the wrong things.

2. My Clarity

Know thyself. This is the reflective gut check phase of delegation that challenges most entrepreneurs. Once we begin to delegate and start to feel the impact, it becomes so liberating that we just want to shed more, more, and more! Finally, we have space to think and create, and we've taught ourselves how to hand things off with ease. Remember the kid in the candy store example? This is the regulation phase that can feel very confining once we've experienced all the freedom that comes with letting go.

Having clarity on what you want to hand off and why is a critical habit to master. It helps us select and commit to only our best ideas. It requires us to sit with an idea for long enough to identify what success looks like and why it's important to our vision in the first place. This habit allows us to improve our overall success rate with delegation, because we set clear expectations around deliverables and outcomes before we run off to the next idea. The best leaders master this skill with intention for the greater good of their vision.

Score Yourself: _____

10	9 8 7	6 5 4	3 2 1
I always stop to get clear on what success looks like before I start to delegate. I keep my team focused on our most impactful work and commit to always set clear expectations for turnaround time and deliverables.	I sometimes delegate on the fly but typically take a minute to prepare my own thoughts around what success looks like before I hand things off. Most of the time, I'm clear about expectations and when things are due.	I rarely stop to think through desired outcomes before I delegate. I will share a few light instructions, but sometimes I forget what I delegated and why. I rarely follow up to see if the tasks are ever completed.	I tend to delegate impulsively on the fly and expect my team to drop everything and read my mind as I hand things off. I don't communicate my expectations on final deliverable or when it needs to be returned to me.

3. My Focus

The third leverage habit to master is our ability to stay focused. When we think of delegation as an Energy Management System™ and we are clear on our vision, we can easily spot the energy drains in our day. For entrepreneurial leaders, this habit can feel so confining to our ability to flow and move from idea to activity with ease. I like to compare it to a fish swimming down a chute. I like the guardrails of a well-planned week, but I need the freedom to flow within those rails.

Being a focused leader is about having a plan and strategy for how we are spending our time that works for us and serves our vision. It's about taking a planful, intentional breath before we dive headfirst into our week. It's about applying some structure to our calendars that gives us space to create, but also accomplish our most important work.

A focused leader starts their week by doing a mix of the following:

- Revisiting their why as well as their most impactful contribution and goals for the quarter, month, and week. Making sure there is time set aside on their calendar to work on activities that support the goal for each time period.

- Understanding and staying attuned to their energy flow.

- Anticipating (preferably with the help of a support partner) what is coming in the week or weeks ahead and planning for it, including delegations.

- Recapping their "must accomplish" list for the day or the week and ensuring they have time blocked on their calendar to make it happen.

- Committing to shut things down based on their other interests and pattern of energy levels. This allows them to rejuvenate their energy for the future. *For me, this is nights and weekends.*

- Articulating their plan for their time to their teams clearly.

  ▷ *Bonus 1: Try to corral your meetings to one or two days a week, and group them by energy level.*

  ▷ *Bonus 2: Have your support partner confirm all meetings for you the day prior and include time blocks before and after to download any important next steps.*

  ▷ *Bonus 3: Pick a system that works for you. I use iCal and a paper planner, which sits under my arm throughout the day.*

Score Yourself: _____

10	9 8 7	6 5 4	3 2 1
I move through my days with a focused, proactive plan that I review weekly. I use time blocking to map out my time for the top things I must accomplish. My team is clear on what I am spending my time on and why.	I start most weeks with a basic plan for the things I must accomplish. I dabble in time blocking and am moderately organized with my time. Sometimes my team pulls me into things that aren't the best use of my time.	I start most weeks wanting to have a basic plan in place. My team still involves me in things they could solve themselves. I find systems, planning, and time blocking to be rigid, and I naturally want to resist them.	I live in a constant state of reaction most days. I don't think I'm good at planning. My team is endlessly involving me in the day-to-day. When I look back at my week, I feel like I didn't do anything impactful.

4. My Value

You will get stuck on this habit if you don't have a sense of what your purpose and contribution are. If you've created a mindset for yourself up to this point where you are attributing your value to how busy you are, how many hats you wear, or how many fires you put out each day, shifting those things off your plate could make you feel bored and useless, if you don't properly understand your own value and contribution.

Idle hands are the devil's workshop, and our own discomfort with feeling "bored" will only create an opportunity to refill the freed-up time with lower-value work, because we are comfortable there. The best way to unpack this is to continue to run exercises around how we *are* spending our time as opposed to how we *want* to spend our time, and what it's costing us to ignore it.

Score Yourself: _____

10	9 8 7	6 5 4	3 2 1
I understand the value of my time. I track and reflect on it regularly. I often run a cost-analysis exercise to see where I may be doing work I don't like or am not good at, and then I look for a way to stop doing it.	I have spent some time thinking about how I want to and am spending my time. I know that my time is worth more than many of the activities that I am doing but haven't done much to address it in an impactful way.	I should evaluate how I'm spending my time. The work I do each day isn't moving the needle for me or my business. Most of what I'm doing could be done better by someone else, but I don't know what I'd do otherwise.	I've never really thought about what the value of my time is. I have not looked at what it costs me to keep doing work I'm not good at and don't like. I don't spend any time reflecting or trying to solve this.

5. My Commitment

This is the hardest habit to master because it requires sustained, continual effort. Once the initial shiny fun of chasing a new habit wears off, we can quickly become bored and move onto the next fun idea, and we've all done it! It's easier to fall back on our limiting beliefs when this happens and allow ourselves to create excuses for why we can't see things through.

When you start to view delegation as an Energy Management System™, it becomes easy for you to shift your mindset from "delegation is a chore" to "delegation is a choice." It's a crucial lever that we can pull to take back our time and energy by handing things off. If you need an extra boost of accountability with this step, try using the habit trackers on our website letitgodelegationbook.com.

Score Yourself: _____

10	9 8 7	6 5 4	3 2 1
I am committed to how I spend my time and energy. I recognize beliefs that may distract me from living my best self. I'm committed to getting my team what they need to do a great job and bring my vision to life.	I want to make a few changes with how I'm spending my time and energy. I know the underlying thoughts that keep me doing busy work, but I don't know what to do about them. I want to let go and see what my team can do.	I know that I'm not contributing my best each day, but I'm comfortable with that. I don't see a lot of changes that I want to make about my time and energy, and don't trust my team to execute as I expect if I let go.	I don't see any issues with how I'm spending my time and don't want to make any changes. I actually enjoy that my team relies on me to come in to save the day all of the time, even if I'm not contributing my best.

THE FIVE MINDSETS

Now let's explore the mindsets that must exist for us to find true leverage. As you know from Part 1, mindset is a way of thinking—an attitude or opinion, especially a habitual one. Our mindset is what we tell ourselves that we perceive as true, and we are what we believe. To shift our reality, we must first shift our awareness, our core beliefs, and our mindset. What we can see, we can be.

In each of the mindsets that follow, think honestly about where you are *currently* with each.

1. I Am Accountable

Creating a culture of accountability must start from the top as we lead by example. Being willing to give and receive feedback in a healthy, objective way is a skill that can take years to master, and is one of the biggest challenges leaders face when it comes to delegation. Accountability means not only doing what we say, but being available to give and receive feedback. Sometimes, we simply don't have enough time to be responsive to our team. This is a great opportunity to create a reliable feedback loop that we can commit to, and set up our delegations for success from the beginning. By communicating our expectations and aligning on timelines when we start the delegation process, and then agreeing to and prioritizing a meeting to sync or communicate progress, we are setting ourselves up for success.

Score Yourself: _____

10	9	8	7	6	5	4	3	2	1
I have created a culture of accountability across my team. I'm willing and comfortable to be held accountable and have a reliable accountability loop and systems for my team. My team also holds each other accountable.	I am working toward a culture of accountability. We have a moderately healthy environment for feedback, and my immediate team is fairly comfortable giving me feedback and holding me accountable when needed.			I have created mild levels of accountability within my company. The team will sometimes speak up and give feedback, but there is no system or loop in place to consistently hold me or them accountable for their work.			I don't want to be held accountable or follow a system of accountability. I don't have time to give or receive feedback with my team and I know they would not be comfortable trying to hold me or each other accountable.		

2. I Am Evaluative

At my company, we run our business using scorecards. Each department has a scorecard and metrics they are accountable for. We review those scorecards weekly and they allow us to better predict and adjust in the moment, rather than live in a constant space of reflection. The same principle can be applied to delegation, especially to larger projects. When you set out to hand something off to your team, take an extra minute to identify a few predictive leading indicators of success. Taking an evaluative approach to delegation allows you to reflect and provide feedback objectively. It also makes it easier to spot and anticipate delays or breakdowns earlier.

What follows are a few examples of success metrics you can use when you delegate.

Sample Sales Goal Success Metric

* Your goal is to increase your business by 25 percent this year. You do that by meeting with people, forming relationships, and keeping connected to them.

  ▷ Your to-do items: Create a list of people, attend the lunch meeting with them, inform your assistant of how it went, and communicate any next steps.

  ▷ Your assistant's to-do items: Contact people about scheduling, make reservations, follow up with clients, and help you execute on any outstanding next steps.

  ▷ The success metric would be to identify how many people you need to meet with each week based on your average close ratio to meet your 25 percent goal. Each week in your meeting, you track against that metric to ensure you stay on target.

Sample Service Goal Success Metric

* Measure client satisfaction through ongoing surveys.

▷ Your to-do items: Create a list of questions, determine frequency, and provide a list of customers to send them to for feedback.

▷ Your assistant's to-do items: Create a form survey with questions, send it out to customers, set up automation, track the information coming in, and report results to the client every day, week, and month.

▷ The success metric would be to track the number of surveys sent per week.

Score Yourself: _____

10	9 8 7	6 5 4	3 2 1
I use metrics to predict, evaluate, and reflect on our success and create objective accountability. I have clear communication systems in place to discuss any breakdowns so that we can learn from them and get better.	I have established a few key metrics that are objective and predictive. I periodically reflect on them but haven't really used them to establish objective accountability. We sometimes discuss breakdowns to get better.	I am working on identifying some key metrics that are objective and predictive. We haven't spent any time creating accountability or reflecting on them yet. We do not discuss breakdowns to learn from them or improve.	I don't have any key objective metrics established with my team and don't know where to start. I haven't spent any time evaluating metrics, and I do not address any breakdowns with my team when things go wrong.

3. I Am Intentional

In the delegation framework, being intentional is about tempering yourself for the greater good of your vision. When you are intentional, you are choosing to share and take action on what's most important to you. You take the time to get really clear up front about what outcome you want to see before you set it in motion.

Understanding and reminding ourselves that our teams live in *execution* while we live in *ideation* is part of being an intentional leader. These competing mindsets can create chaos and overwhelm our teams as they are trying to focus on our established priorities. A company with endlessly distracted leadership cannot contribute in meaningful ways or sustain growth over time. Your intentional commitment not to chase shiny objects when things get hard creates a culture of focus and discipline.

Score Yourself: _____

10	9	8	7	6	5	4	3	2	1
I only share and execute my best ideas. I'm intentional with what I share—my team lives in execution while I live in ideation. These competing mindsets can overwhelm my team as they work on established priorities.		I catch myself now that I understand that my team acts on all of my ideas. I try to temper myself with what I share, and I created some systems to capture my ideas so I don't distract from our established priorities.			I am willing to make some changes when it comes to how and when I share my new ideas with my team. I haven't really established a system to keep my thoughts organized, but I want to try so I can keep them focused.			Ideating is what makes me special, and my team just needs to keep up. They can figure out how to prioritize what's on their plates. My fresh ideas are what keep us relevant and fresh, and I share them all the time.	

4. I Am Realistic

As a chronic time optimist, this mindset is one that I always struggle with. I recognize that sometimes my energy for my ideas does not match my team's capacity to execute well, and if I'm not careful, I can break them. Sometimes, even the best laid delegations break down. So, with this mindset, it's about controlling what you can to expect a reliable outcome. This mindset involves a commitment to always have a conversation about a realistic completion timeline with the person you are delegating to. This ensures you're both on the same page.

In that conversation, you'll likely set a few success metrics and lay down the framework for a communication cadence that works for you both. Then, you recap what's been discussed: "Okay, Georgia, you're going to do XYZ by Tuesday, and when you're done, you'll message me. Once I take a look and make my edits, you can schedule it to go out." By verbally recapping what you are both agreeing to, it allows the other person to hear what you perceive the plan to be and respond in the moment. *Bonus points for including success metrics: If something starts to go off track, we will know because of the XYZ success metric, and our backup plan is to do XYZ.*

Score Yourself: _____

10	9	8	7	6	5	4	3	2	1
I am realistic with how long things take when they are delegated. I have clear communication systems in place to ensure we are all clear on who is doing what by when and if the timing or process needs to be changed.	I sometimes underestimate how long things take and if my team has the bandwidth. I try to align with my team when I delegate. They know they can just reach out, but we don't have great communication all of the time.			I acknowledge that it is really hard for me to be on the same page with my team regarding how long things might take to complete. I tend to delegate quickly without making sure we are aligned on timing or process.			I love being a Quickstart and know that I can be totally unrealistic when setting timelines with my team. I don't have time to sync with them about what they might be working on or brainstorm when things break down.		

5. I Am Supportive

This is my favorite mindset to develop because it's where the magic starts to happen. As we try to implement a culture of delegation within our company that starts with us, it's important to remember that our teams are likely *scared* to delegate some of their own tasks. This may come as a surprise to you, but they are not used to having the freedom, autonomy, or permission to hand things off their plates. And if they see us projecting our value based upon how much our hair is on fire on any given day, what example are we creating for them? If we want to create elevated, high-performing teams, we must lead the charge by valuing our own time, teaching them how to do the same, and providing them with the tools and resources to do it well.

Score Yourself: _____

10	9	8	7	6	5	4	3	2	1
I empower my team with the tools, permission, feedback and autonomy to always do their highest and best work. I am committed to seeing everyone doing their highest and best work because it elevates us as a team.	I really want everyone doing their highest and best work because it helps us elevate as a team, but we aren't there yet. I want to provide them with the tools, resources, and autonomy they need to elevate themselves.			I think I could do a better job supporting my team to do their highest and best work. I've given them general permission to delegate, but they have neither the tools nor the resources, nor do they have anyone to delegate to.			I think my team is scared to delegate. They tie their contributions to how busy they are and worry their roles may become obsolete. They could be more fulfilled if I permitted them to work on higher-value activities.		

TOTAL SCORE: _____

No matter where you fall in the scorecard, approaching your delegation practice in this objective way as you start to execute helps you pinpoint trouble spots that might be holding you back from fully letting go. Or inversely, it helps you recognize habits or mindsets that you can amplify further to create more of the space you seek.

After a few months of focusing on delegation, retake the assessment and track and celebrate progress. Have your team score you or let them score themselves and evaluate where they are strong or want to improve their time. And, speaking of your team, let's explore how you can use what you've learned about delegation and apply it across your entire company.

RECAP

1. Let's recap and build on what we've covered in this chapter. The mindset or habit that I struggle with the most is

   _____,

   and I think that's because of _____

   _____.

2. The mindset or habit that I excel at the most is

   _____,

   and I think that's because of _____

   _____.

3. I commit to improve on my _____ habit or mindset by doing _____.

4. The affirmation that I will repeat to myself when I start to feel negatively about letting go is: _____
_____

In the next chapter we'll go deeper into how to leverage a culture of delegation to elevate yourself, your team, and your company.

CHAPTER 9

CASCADING A CULTURE OF DELEGATION

"Culture eats strategy for breakfast."

—PETER DRUCKER

I got the chance to sit with Tom about a year and a half after his weekend at the cabin. I was proud of him for taking the step to focus on himself and find his vision, and enjoyed watching him rise to the occasion to lead. That weekend had been transformational for him, and I was excited to hear about the steps he'd taken since then to elevate his time.

"The company I'm running now looks nothing like the business I stepped into," he told me proudly. "Sure, we build and sell the same things that we did when my dad was in charge, and he was a genius at that, but it's an entirely different company culture now. My time is just about fully spent doing what I envisioned—coaching and elevating my team—and I'm energized every day by it. Our culture still has the rugged elements of 'carry your own bag' from my father's era, but the team now is clear on what their most impactful 'bag' actually is. They are deeply connected to and motivated by our core purpose, and now know why they want to carry it and how their responsibilities impact our entire team's ability to achieve great things."

Tom was living out the vision he had seen for himself back at the cabin. His most impactful contribution was being able to coach his team to excellence to create a winning culture of people doing work they love and are great at. Revenues were up, profits were up, and the team was also earning more than ever due to an amazing profit-sharing program that Tom had engineered.

I asked him how he was able to accomplish so much in such a short period of time. He reflected for a bit and then said, "**I set the vision and then got out of everyone's way.** I knew that for us to achieve the greatness I could see ahead for us, I had to lead by example. I had to be the one to first boldly say, 'This is what I know I'm here to do, this is my vision, and I need your help and support to get us where we need to be.' From there, I just worked tirelessly at letting go with Anne and my team, getting out of their way, cheering them on, and staying in my lane."

In just a year and a half, Tom had achieved his vision for how he was spending his time. His ability to visibly elevate himself as the leader, along with his relentless encouragement, gave his team the confidence and permission to do the same.

And you can too. Imagine arriving at work, and everyone on your team is spending the majority of their time doing their most impactful work. They are in the right seats and doing work that energizes and excites them. Your employee retention is up, your client retention is up. Your organization is creating value you never even thought possible because your team's energy is tripled. You've given them the permission, autonomy, and resources to think creatively in their roles to solve problems, create new service lines, and spend time doing more of what they love and less of what they don't.

Delegation *is* the foundation for limitless growth. It's the most important tool you can leverage to get your team and your company from where you are today to your greatest vision of success.

TEACH DELEGATION
BY EXAMPLE

Let's talk about the dynamics of delegation, because you will no doubt face opposition for taking such a bold position to get everyone delegating, especially if the culture is contrary to this. At one of my favorite entrepreneurial coaching programs, Strategic Coach™, we are taught that as entrepreneurs we live in a risk economy. The more risk, the greater the possible reward. Our teams conversely live in a safety economy. They value the safety and security of their job. Introducing a culture of delegation could initially create a lot of anxiety and fear around their own value and contribution, because they are likely subconsciously aware that they need to stay and look busy to prove valuable. So, this is a culture shift that stems from *you* leading by example and creating a safe environment for them to let go without fear of losing their jobs.

You will need to teach them by example and build trust, so that they are encouraged to delegate their lower-impact work. Coach them to have a vision around their highest and best contribution. You'll need to invest in resources to support the work that is shed, or in technologies that can do things faster than a human can. In this culture, you keep driving the work further and further down or out of the organization, and then just get out of the way. A culture of delegation rewards this "elevation" thinking because it means that we have our best people mentally freed up to work on our most impactful issues and projects that will drive the business forward.

Some truths to keep in mind as you embark on this journey:

- The world is not full of visionaries like you. Your team is likely *not* filled with visionaries. You can only have one visionary in the company, but your team can be visionary about improving things on the ground level. And, they can still make a lasting impact through their work. They can be clear about what impact they want to make as individuals doing this work. When encouraged, they can bring vision to how they can best spend their time within the constructs of their jobs.

* This will initially be scary for all involved. For you, the fear is around allowing your team to systematically let go and accepting the potential initial outlay costs that might come from green lighting a delegation program. You may have to pay for extra resources to get your team better leveraged. You may lose team members who are comfortable with the status quo and don't want to let go of their work. Until this moment of you making this bold leadership shift, you have created and led by example a culture of *busy=productive*. Your team will absolutely be scared of a new dynamic of *impact=value*.

* This approach is not the current business norm, and that's okay. Our culture of eight to five, seated at a desk making sure you look busy when the boss walks by, is shifting. People want autonomy. They want to do work that fits into their lives. They want to make both money and an impact doing work they enjoy. They want to feel like they are making a difference and want to be motivated by their work. Embracing this different way of working is an opportunity to shine as a leader in your space and create a company that is thriving and making a difference to the clients you serve and the team you employ.

- This is a massive shift in how you operate, and it's not an overnight transformation. This is a long-haul commitment to change the way our organizations attribute value and contribution. Because the root of how we value our time is so ingrained into our work cultures, our metrics, our management styles, and even our job descriptions, this is a day-by-day battle to change hearts and minds that you ultimately must be committed to. When you embrace this philosophy, wrong-fit team members will begin to surface. Those who are comfortable with and prefer the busy work will become uncomfortable with this shift, which could lead to turnover. All of this will cull your staff into one that lives and dies by the impact they can make.

EXECUTING A CULTURE
OF DELEGATION

Here's how to roll out an elevation program of delegation in your company from a tactical standpoint.

- Start at the top. Encourage your leadership team to continually identify at least 10 to 25 percent of their work each quarter that can be delegated.

- Then, cascade down to the management team level. Encourage them to delegate as many business and personal tasks as possible to subordinates with available bandwidth.

- Next, move to your sales and service teams. Press them to identify at least 10 percent of their work that they can delegate to newer team members. Use some of these tasks as part of your hands-on exposure training for new hires.

- Integrate an outsourced resource to assist when there is overflow or not enough capacity on your existing team to support the delegation.

- At my company, we've even financially supported our team by encouraging them to delegate personal home responsibilities such as house cleaning, meal delivery, and grocery shopping. Think whole-person as you create your elevation program.

- Create ghost seats on your accountability chart as you all start to shed tasks and need to create new roles within. Start to envision in advance the next *who* that needs to be added to the team, and thoughtfully build toward that.

- Have everyone on your team use a simple delegation template that forces them to think through a delegation thoughtfully and create alignment on who is doing what by when. *(There is an example template on our website at letitgodelegationbook.com.)*

In my business, the more that I can elevate my team out of the mundane tasks, the more deeply they can work with our clients. This increases our overall impact as an organization because we can have them focus more on helping clients find more freedom, which is part of our company vision.

When it comes to elevating your teams, the approach is the same thought process you followed. You'll begin to teach from day one that they are here to create as much impact for you as possible. Teach them to be clear and aligned with who they are, and clear on the absolute best use of their time within their role.

STEPS TO ROLLOUT

Follow these steps as you work to roll out delegation with each of your team members:

1. First, help them gain clarity on what their most impactful contributions are and could be by using the exercises from earlier chapters, as well as this tool, built just for your team. Have them complete the Elevated Week Exercise that is found on our website at letitgodelegationbook.com.

2. Compare that against their job description and ensure they are in the right seat, and that the impact they want to create aligns with your vision for the organization.

a. Example: If someone is in a service seat and they want to create an impact in sales outreach, they are not aligned. Do not pass go, their role and seat need to be reevaluated.

b. If they are in the service seat and they say that the impact they want to make is to help as many clients as possible achieve XYZ of the service they are performing, then they need to be freed up to do so.

3. Set some metrics and next steps around what can reasonably come off their plates in the next quarter.

4. Give them the autonomy, permission, and resources to actually delegate. Utilize tools like the Delegate Freedom System™ so that they are delegating effectively and efficiently.

5. Create an offload plan for how and to whom work is being transferred. Measure the success and impact with regularity (at least every quarter). Just keep systematically driving the busy work down throughout the organization until there are no levels left on your accountability chart to drive it to, and then it's time to outsource.

BALANCING COMPANY
NEEDS WITH JOBS

On the subject of balancing the needs of the company with the jobs people were hired to do, my philosophy is this: a team doing work they love and are excited about creates the most impactful, progressive, and ambitious organization filled with happy, satisfied employees and thereby raving fan clients. There is nothing more impactful than having the right people in the right seats elevating themselves to their greatest contribution.

As you create a culture of delegation, and encourage people to let go, your job is to teach your team to protect their newfound time with intentionality. Help them identify what their most impactful contribution should be, and then simply get out of the way.

A CASCADE, NOT A DELUGE

It's important to remember that creating a culture of delegation takes time and should happen thoughtfully. As you begin to elevate your time, your team will be on the receiving end of all the delegations coming off your plate. As you cascade this mindset throughout your organization, the work will naturally begin to come off everyone's plates. Start with your leadership team. The deeper you go into the organization, the more aware you must become of how much delegation and capacity your team is equipped to handle.

As entrepreneurs, we tend to decide, commit, and do. Just remain aware of the flow of work that might be accumulating on others' plates as a result of your commitment to delegation. Take your time, and pace this out thoughtfully every step of the way. What feels energizing and like more freedom to you will likely equate to more work for others, who may have very full plates already.

I recommend starting with a goal of everyone on your leadership team finding 10 percent of work that they can delegate. As you master 10 percent, increase to 15 percent, then 20 percent, and then 25 percent, quarter over quarter.

Lead by example, and commit to making this exercise part of any regular quarterly conversations your teams are having. Always keep in mind the goal of having clarity on what your team will do with the newly found time. As the leadership team is elevating, begin having these same conversations with the next level of the organization. When done thoughtfully and carefully, you'll find your team to be energized by the shifts and efforts being made to free them up to make their most impactful contribution.

CONCLUSION

Letting go of work that doesn't serve you or your vision is the number one goal I want you to take away from this book. Your ability to shift your mindset, technique, and execution with delegation is what will get you from where you are now to where you want to be.

As we saw with Tom, as he began to gain clarity for himself on the impact he was destined to make, he was able to let go and get out of the way of his team and let everyone do their best work.

Start by visualizing what you want for yourself in terms of how you are spending your time. Get clear on the most impactful contribution you bring to the world, and follow the system I've presented to get the work off your plate that doesn't support your vision. Then, teach and empower your team to elevate their time. You can do it. Your contribution to this process is crucial. You have the tools and learnings you need now to finally master delegation and become an awesome delegator!

(i) All the resources you need can be found on our website at <u>letitgo</u> <u>delegationbook.com</u>.

I'd love to hear from you about the wins you've been able to achieve on your delegation journey.

This book has been a labor of love for me. It is the culmination of more than fifteen years of working alongside entrepreneurs at all phases of their delegation journey. I deeply understand and relate to your struggles and triumphs with delegation. As I was writing this book, I was constantly fencing off self-sabotaging thoughts and holding myself to the highest standard of leading by example. I continually asked myself if my team and I were practicing what I preach. I can assure you that I'm not perfect, and that my team is not perfect. I'm a genetically wired eternal time optimist who can still get in my own way and my team's way by holding on to work that I should let go.

I continue to learn and recognize that this work we do as bold leaders is about striving for self-mastery. This is about taking steps that inch us closer to our ideal, which is a horizon that we will never quite reach. There's always further to go, which is why it's so important that we acknowledge and celebrate our wins and pull our teams up with us. We must bolster our confidence with affirmations and continually recommit to the hard work that true excellence in leadership requires. I hold myself and my team, as a delegation company, to the highest example of this, and I am continually striving alongside you, chasing down that horizon.

I wish you amazing success on your elevation journey, and I will be watching from the sidelines in awe of your most impactful contribution, as you finally gain the time and space to *Let It Go.*

CPSIA information can be obtained
at www.ICGtesting.com
Printed in the USA
BVHW040947120822
644446BV00012B/228/J